I0828788

ILLUSTRATED CATALOGUE

OF THE

MUSEUM OF COMPARATIVE ZOÖLOGY,

AT HARVARD COLLEGE.

Published by order of the Legislature of Massachusetts.

No. III.

MONOGRAPH OF THE NORTH AMERICAN ASTACIDÆ.

BY

DR. HERMANN A. HAGEN.

CAMBRIDGE:
FOR SALE BY SEVER AND FRANCIS.
1870.

University Press: Welch, Bigelow, & Co.,
Cambridge.

NOTE.

IT is but justice to DR. HAGEN to state that this monograph was completed by him and handed to me for publication as early as October, 1868. Circumstances over which I had no control have delayed its passage through the press till now.

LOUIS AGASSIZ.

CAMBRIDGE, February 21, 1870.

CONTENTS.

EXPLANATION OF THE PLATES.

Plate I. First abdominal legs of the male.

C. acutus, Form I., fig. 1 in front; fig. 2 outside. Form II., fig. 4 in front; fig. 3 the same enlarged; fig. 5 outside.

C. Clarkii, Form I., fig. 7 in front; fig. 8 outside. Form II., fig. 9 in front; fig. 10 outside.

C. troglodytes, Form I., fig. 11 in front; fig. 12 outside. Form II., fig. 13 in front; fig. 14 outside.

C. Lecontei, Form I., fig. 15 in front; fig. 16 outside. Form II., fig. 17 in front; fig. 18 outside.

C. affinis, Form I., fig. 19 in front; fig. 20 outside. Form II., fig. 21 in front; fig. 22 outside.

C. virilis, Form I, fig. 23 in front; fig. 24 outside; figs. 25, 26 varieties outside. Form II, fig 27 in front; fig. 28 outside.

C. juvenilis, Form I., fig. 29 in front; fig. 30 outside; fig. 31 viewed more outwardly. Form II., fig. 32 in front; fig. 33 outside.

C. propinquus, Form I., fig. 34 in front; fig. 35 variety; fig. 36 outside. Form II., fig. 37 in front; fig. 38 outside.

C. obesus, Form I., fig. 39 in front; fig 40 outside. Form II., fig. 41 in front; fig. 42 outside.

C. latimanus, Form I., fig. 43 in front; fig. 44 outside. Form II., fig. 45 in front; fig. 46 outside.

C. Bartonii, Form I., fig. 47 in front; fig. 48 outside. Form II., fig. 49 in front; fig. 50 outside.

C. Carolinus, Form I., fig. 51 in front; fig. 52 outside. Form II., fig. 53 in front; fig. 54 outside.

C. versutus, Form I., fig. 55 in front; fig. 56 outside. Form II., fig. 57 in front; fig. 58 outside.

C. spiculifer, Form I., fig. 59 in front; fig. 60 outside. Form II., fig. 61 in front; fig. 62 outside.

C. Blandingii (Type), Form I., fig. 63 in front; fig. 64 outside.

C. angustatus (Type), Form I., fig. 65 in front; fig. 66 outside; fig. 67 inside.

C. pellucidus, Form I., fig. 68 in front; fig. 69 outside. Form II., fig. 70 in front; fig. 71 outside.

C. obscurus, Form I., fig. 72 in front; fig. 73 outside. Form II., fig. 74 in front; fig. 75 outside.

C. placidus, Form I., fig. 76 in front; fig. 77 outside. Form II., fig. 78 in front; fig. 79 outside.

C. rusticus, Form I., fig. 80 in front; fig. 81 outside. Form II., fig. 82 in front; fig. 83 outside.

C. affinis, very old (*C. Pealei*), Form I., fig. 84 in front; fig. 85 outside.

C. lancifer, Form I., fig. 86 in front; fig. 87 outside.

C. extraneus, Form II., fig. 88 in front; fig. 89 outside.

C. advena, Form I., fig. 90 in front; fig. 91 enlarged in front; fig. 92 outside.

C. penicillatus, Form I., fig. 93 in front; fig. 94 outside. Form II., fig. 95 in front; fig. 96 outside.

A. Gambelii, fig. 97 in front; fig. 98 outside.

C. Clarkii (Type), young, Form II., fig. 99 in front; fig. 100 outside.

C. immunis, Form I., fig. 101 in front; fig. 102 outside.

C. fallax, Form I., fig. 103 in front; fig. 104 outside; fig. 105 inside.

Plate II.

C. acutus, Form I., fig. 106 in front; fig. 108 outside. Var. A, Form. I., fig. 107 in front; fig. 109 outside.

Form II. (young 1.7 inch long), fig. 110 outside; (2.7 inch long) fig. 111 outside.

Form II. (2.7 inch long) fig. 112 outside, imperfectly articulated.

Form II. (4.4 inch long), fig. 113 outside, not articulated.

Ventre between the fourth legs of the female, fig. 114; the same in var. A, fig. 115.

Rostrum from above, fig. 116; var. A, fig. 117.

Epistoma, fig. 118; var. A, fig. 119.

C. acutus, Transverse line of the thorax, fig. 124 ; var. A, fig. 125.

Inner sexual parts of the Male Form I., fig. 120 ; testicules viewed from above, fig. 121. Form II., fig. 122.

Inner sexual parts of the female, fig. 123.

Annulus ventralis of the female, fig. 126 ; the same, inner side, fig. 127.

C. Clarkii, development of the first abdominal leg in the male, 0.3 inch long, fig. 133 ; the knob enlarged, fig. 134.

C. virilis, inner sexual parts of the Male Form I., fig. 128 ; side, fig. 129 ; testicules viewed from above, fig. 132.

The same, in Form II., fig. 130 ; side, fig. 131.

C. Bartonii, inner sexual parts of the Male Form I., fig. 135 ; side, fig. 136.

The same in Form II., fig 137 ; side, fig. 138.

Inner sexual parts of the female, fig. 139.

Plate III. *a*, lamina antennalis ; *b*, epistoma ; *c*, the exterior spine of the second joint of the exterior antenna. (The letters are only indicated in fig. 140.)

CAMBARUS. GROUP I.

C. Blandingii (Type), fig. 140. *C. troglodytes*, fig. 141. *C. Clarkii*, fig. 142. *C. acutus*, fig. 143. *C. acutus*, var. B, fig. 144. *C. Lecontei*, fig. 145. *C. angustatus* (Type), fig. 146. *C. spiculifer*, fig. 147. *C. pellucidus*, fig. 148. *C. penicillatus*, fig. 149, *C. versutus*, fig. 150. *C. Wiegmanni*, fig. 151.

CAMBARUS. GROUP II.

C. affinis, fig. 152. *C. propinquus*, fig. 153. *C. obscurus*, fig. 154. *C. virilis*, fig. 155. *C. extraneus*, fig. 156. *C. juvenilis*, fig. 157. *C. placidus*, fig. 158. *C. lancifer*, fig. 159. *C. immunis*, fig. 160 ; fig. *d*, var. of the epistoma. *C. rusticus*, fig. 161.

CAMBARUS. GROUP III.

C. latimanus, fig. 162. *C. obesus*, fig. 163. *C. advena*, fig. 164. *C. Carolinus*, fig. 165. *C. Bartonii*, fig. 166. *C. robustus*, fig. 167.

ASTACUS.

A. nigrescens, fig. 168. *A. Klamathensis*, fig. 169. *A. Gambelii*, fig. 170. *A. Trowbridgii*, fig. 171.

Plate IV.

Cambarus Clarkii, Male Form I. (nat. size).

Plate V.

Cambarus *affinis*, Fem. (nat. size).

Plate VI.

Cambarus pellucidus, Male Form I. (nat. size).

Plate VII.

Cambarus advena, Male Form I. (twice enlarged).

Plate VIII.

Cambarus virilis, Male Form I. (nat. size) ; a hand of var. A. *Cambarus immunis*, hand.

Plate IX.

Cambarus obesus, Male Form I. (nat. size).

Plate X.

Astacus Trowbridgii, Fem. Type (nat. size).

Plate XI.

Astacus Gambelii, Male. Type (nat. size).

INTRODUCTION.

THE following monograph of the Fresh-water Crawfishes of North America is intended to form the first step in a scientific examination of the rich crustacean materials contained in the Museum of Comparative Zoölogy at Harvard College, in Cambridge. The excellent monograph of the genus Callinectes, published by Mr. A. Ordway in 1863, is the only work about Crustacea, based principally upon the Cambridge collection.

Arriving in Cambridge in October, 1867, in order to take care of the articulated animals belonging to the Museum, I was charged first to arrange and put in order the Crustacea. Because of the almost total lack of room and of working hands (the rich collections from Brazil procured by the Thayer Expedition having occupied all working time for the last two years), but a small part had been as yet determined and arranged in the rooms opened for public exhibition. The greater portion of them had been stored for several years in the cellar, and therefore was so situated as not to be readily accessible for a scientific examination.

The part exhibited comprised a series of three hundred and twenty-seven determined species in a systematical collection, also three hundred and thirty-seven determined species in several faunal collections, and a few types of the United States Exploring Expedition. Nearly all the latter species being represented also in the systematical series, the number of named species (determined mostly by Mr. Dana and Mr. W. Stimpson) did not perhaps exceed five hundred. With the exception of several boxes already separated, with duplicates for exchange, they answered to a catalogue of nearly sixteen hundred numbers, containing the names of the respective localities and collectors, the dates of capture, and, in some cases, the scientific determinations by Mr. W. Stimpson.

The whole collection is now in a safe condition, mostly unpacked and arranged in new alcohol. The division of the entire assemblage has been carried as far as the families, that of the greater part as far as the genera, while several families have been critically identified. There are over four thousand two hundred jars. The number of specimens, perhaps, exceeds sixty thousand; the additions during the years 1863–1866 were fourteen thousand specimens. According to Professor L. Agassiz's estimate, the collection comprises more than two thousand species, the entire number of species as yet known being about five thousand. A closer examination of several families verifies this estimate, or rather indicates that it is probably too small. Nearly one half of the collection is formed by the Brachyura, one fourth by the Macroura.

The value of the collection is the greater from the circumstance that most of it has been secured and formed, in view of a definite plan adopted by Professor L. Agassiz for the purpose of examining and defining the different faunæ in the gigantic water-area spreading between the coast of Eastern Africa and Western America. Several persons have been charged with the collecting of the fishes, the crustacea, and the polyps at chosen points, — at Zanzibar, Mr. C. Cooke; at Kingsmills, Sandwich and Society Islands, Mr. Garrett; on the West Coast of America, Messrs. A. Agassiz, and T. G. Cary. At the same time rich collections have been received from additional intermediate localities,— Rangoon, Singapore, China, New Holland, and others, chiefly through Captain W. A. Putnam. The Museum is also very rich in specimens from the shores of the United States, from the Antilles, and from Brazil; it likewise possesses valuable materials from the European and Mediterranean fauna.

The materials examined by me for this monograph of the North American Astacidæ are, I think, as yet unrivalled. They consist of the following assemblages: 1. The Astacidæ of the Cambridge Museum, twenty-five species, represented by nearly two thousand alcoholic specimens from one hundred and fifty different collectors and as many different localities, besides some dry specimens, partly types of Dr. Gibbes. 2. The Astacidæ of the Museum of the Philadelphia Academy, kindly communicated to me by Professor Leidy, containing types of Messrs. John LeConte and Girard. 3. The Astacidæ of the Museum of the Natural History Society in Boston, containing types of Professor W. Stimpson. 4. The Astacidæ of the Museum of the Peabody Academy in Salem, which, with the last, were kindly communicated to me by Dr.

A. S. Packard. 5. Types of nine species of Mr. Girard and Professor W. Stimpson, kindly communicated to me by Professor W. Stimpson.

The Astacidæ in the collection of the Smithsonian Institution I have not yet seen.

I have described thirty-eight species,—thirty-two Cambari and six Astaci. Eleven species, all Cambari, are new. There are six species —four Cambari and two Astaci—which I have not seen.

Among the twenty-eight species of Cambarus which I have examined I have seen the two forms of the male, and the female of twenty-three species, the first form of the male and the female of one species. There are two species, of which I have seen only the first form of the male; of one species I have seen only the second form; of five species I have seen but single specimens; of all others, a considerable number.

Among the four species of Astacus which I have examined I have seen of one species both the male and female; of another species, the male only; of the other two species, the female only; and in all cases only a few specimens of each species.

This monograph, as I am convinced, is very far from embracing the entire number of species living in North America. May new explorations soon render my work incomplete.

HISTORY OF THE AMERICAN ASTACIDÆ.

1798. THE first North American species made known was described by Fabricius, in his *Supplementum Entomologiæ Systematicæ.* It was called *Astacus Bartonii*, and communicated by Professor Smith Barton. The description is very short, and the locality not given, but it is probably the species more recently determined as *A. Bartonii* by American naturalists. Bosc, Hist. Nat. des Crust., Suites à Buffon an x. (1802), describes in few words, repeated by Latreille, Hist. Nat. des Crust., VI. 240, *Astacus Bartonii*, which he collected in America. The figure given by him is very bad, and it is impossible to identify his species.

1817. Rafinesque, in the American Monthly Magazine, II. 42, November, describes four species, — *Astacus limosus*, *fossor*, *ciliaris*, and *pusillus*. His descriptions are likewise very short, but the locality is given, and it will therefore be possible to determine them exactly by further investigations.

A. limosus is perhaps *A. affinis* Say, and *A. fossor* the species described by me as *A. obscurus*, if it has burrowing habits. *A. ciliaris* is apparently *A. Bartonii*, but the dimensions given by Rafinesque are, as for the foregoing species, excessive. The ciliated legs do not belong exclusively to this species. I think *A. pusillus* does not differ from *A. ciliaris*. The differences given are not important, — "the rostrum oval acute," "the hands oblong, dotted," "entirely fulvous brown"; in *A. ciliaris*, "the rostrum short, acute," "the hands short, thick dotted," "entirely olivaceous brown." Perhaps *A. pusillus* is the second form of the male; still, ciliæ always occur on its second pair of legs, and Rafinesque would have mentioned the fact in this instance no less than in *A. ciliaris*.

One month after the appearance of the account of Rafinesque, Th. Say, in Journ. Acad. Phil., I. Part I. 167, December, described two species, — *A. Bartonii* and *affinis*. His descriptions are good, and sufficient to designate the species. A supplement is given, l. c. 443, concerning the variation of their armature and the proportion of the hands in *A. Bartonii*; but here perhaps Mr. Say speaks of a different species. *Astacus Bartonii* Say is probably the species described by Fabricius, and *Astacus affinis* seems to be *Astacus limosus* Rafinesque.

The better description authorizes us to prefer a name published one month later.

1830. R. Harlan, in Trans. Amer. Philos. Soc. Phila. III. 464, gives the description of *Astacus Blandingii* from South Carolina, repeated in 1835 in his Medic. and Phys. Research. 229, with the addition of short specific characters of *Astacus Bartonii* and *affinis*, and the figures of the three species. But the numbers of two species are erroneously changed in the drawings. The specimen types preserved in the collection of the Philadelphia Academy have been kindly communicated to me by Professor Leidy.

1833. John D. Godman, in Rambles of a Naturalist, Philadelphia, pp. 40, 41, has communicated his observations upon the burrowing habits of *Cambarus Diogenes*. I have not seen this work, which is quoted by Mr. Ch. Girard.

1837. Professor Milne-Edwards, of Paris, in his Hist. Nat. des Crust., II. 331, describes *Astacus Bartonii*, *affinis*, and *Chilensis*. The change of the numbers in Harlan's figures has apparently induced him to reverse the names of the two species.

1839. Mr. J. W. Randall, Journ. Acad. Phila., VIII., Part I. 138, describes *Astacus Oreganus* from the Columbia River, figured in pl. 7. The description is very short and the figure apparently very erroneous. The type was lost by the artist, and it is still impossible to identify the species.

1842. De Haan, in Faun. Japonic. Crust., 164, has observed the interesting fact that *Astacus Bartonii* and *A. affinis* possess one gill less than *A. fluviatilis* and *Japonicus*. The gill on the fifth pair of legs is wanting.

Professor Z. Thompson, in his Natural History of Vermont, 170, notes the occurrence of *Astacus Bartonii* in that State.

1844. In J. Mueller, Archiv. 383, Dr. Tellkampf describes the remarkable blind species from the Mammoth Cave in Kentucky, *A. pellucidus*.

James E. De Kay, in his Zoölogy of New York, Part VI., Crustacea, 22, gives the description and figure (pl. 8, fig. 25) of *Astacus Bartonii*, and the diagnoses of *A. affinis*, *Blandingii*, and *Oreganus*.

1845. I. E. Gray published in Journals of Exped. of Discovery in Central Australia, by E. J. Eyre, a paper on some *Astaci* from New Holland, in which he suggests that the genus *Astacus* may be divided into three sections, characterized by the texture of the caudal segment, in being calcareous or not to its top. Mr. James D. Dana has proved that this character cannot be of much value in classification.

1846. Erichson, in Wiegmann's Archiv. Jahrg., XII. 86, and supplement, 375, gives an elaborate monograph of the whole genus *Astacus*. He describes from America, *Astacus pellucidus*, *affinis*, *Carolinus*, *Bar-*

tonii, *Blandingii* (after Harlan's description and figure), *Wiegmanni*, *Mexicanus*, *Cubensis*, *Chilensis* (after M. Edwards's description), and *Oreganus* (after Randall's description and figure). His materials were few; of *A. pellucidus* and *affinis* he saw but one specimen, but his descriptions are largely comparative. The observation first made by De Haan, that the American species possess no gills at the base of the fifth pair of legs, is repeated and verified in the other species described by Erichson, and taken for the formation of a particular subgenus, *Cambarus*. Erichson's monograph is still unrivalled, comprising all the species of the whole world. Still, there is no certainty in the determination of the species which he described, since so many similar species have been more recently found. But it is possible to arrange them in my groups, as Erichson has noted the number of hooked legs of the males. His types are preserved in the Berlin Museum, and an examination of them will prove, perhaps, that in the case of some species my determinations are erroneous.

1850. Mr. Lewis R. Gibbes, in his work "On the Carcinol. Collect. in the U. S.," 31, quoted *Astacus Bartonii*, *affinis*, *Blandingii*, and *pellucidus*. But the localities given by him are doubtful, as I have seen very different species presented by him, under the same name, to the Philadelphia and the Cambridge Museums.

1854. The richness of the materials preserved at the Smithsonian Institution in Washington, and chiefly collected by Professor S. F. Baird, led Mr. Ch. Girard to examine them critically in "A Revision of the North American *Astaci*, with Observations on their Habits and Geographical Distribution," Proc. Acad. Phil., VI. 87, and to characterize them briefly, deferring to another opportunity more full descriptions, accompanied by the necessary illustrations. Mr. Girard enumerates twenty species, eleven of which are new. Two, *C. Oreganus* and *fossor*, he had not seen. Professor Stimpson has kindly communicated to me the types of five of the eleven new species, namely, *C. Clarkii*, *propinquus*, *montanus*, *rusticus*, *longulus*, and the types of two species described before, namely, *A. Bartonii* and *affinis*. The Museum of the Philadelphia Academy possesses also some species labelled with Mr. Girard's names, which were kindly communicated to me by Professor Leidy. I do not know whether these specimens are types, since some are marked with a ?; but as they are mostly from the localities quoted by M. Girard, their identity is probable. These species are: *C. Pealei?* from the Potomac, *C. rusticus?*, *C. montanus?*, *C. Diogenes?* from the District of Columbia, *C. acutissimus* from Kemper County, Missouri, *C. Blandingii* from South Carolina, *C. robustus* from the Humber River at Toronto, *C. propinquus?* from Garrison Creek, Sackett's Harbor, *C. montanus?* from the James River, Virginia. Also, of the twenty species enumerated by Mr. Ch. Girard I have certainly not seen his types of the five following: *C. pellucidus, Carolinus, pusillus, Nebrascensis, acutus,* nor the two species which he had not seen himself, *C. Oreganus* and *fossor.*

Mr. Ch. Girard has adopted the generic name *Cambarus* Erichson for the American species described by him. The introduction to Mr. Ch. Girard's Revision, etc., "according to recent investigations (Erichson is here quoted alone), the crawfishes, or *Astaci,* have been distributed into several genera," does not agree at all with Erichson's words. Erichson, in his monograph, p. 86, in dividing the old genus *Astacus,* expressly says: "The five groups quoted seem to have a higher value than merely subdivisions. Perhaps hereafter they will constitute genera. They may provisionally be regarded as subgenera." Mr. Girard added that Mr. James D. Dana had reclaimed the genus *Astacus* for North America by a species from the Columbia River, — *A. leniusculus.* Subsequently, Proc. Acad. Phil., VI. 375, Professor Agassiz stated that *C. Gambelii,* described as *Cambarus* by Mr. Ch. Girard, possesses six pairs of gills like the crawfishes of Europe, and does not belong to *Cambarus* at all. This statement is the more striking, as Erichson only gives as the character of *Cambarus,* "no gills on the fifth legs." The reply of Mr. Ch. Girard, l. c., p. 381, that he was not satisfied that this peculiarity is of generic value, and consequently that he described *C. Gambelii* as *Cambarus* with the same propriety as he might have placed it in the genus *Astacus,* gives no more light upon the characters of generic value which induced Mr. Ch. Girard to separate *Cambarus* as a distinct genus. In his Revision, etc., nothing more is said concerning this point, and he has not given any other character for his genus *Cambarus,* including *C. Gambelii* and *Oreganus.*

It is to be regretted that Mr. Ch. Girard has not fulfilled his plan of giving more full descriptions, accompanied with the necessary graphic illustrations. His short descriptions are not sufficient to indicate his new species with certainty, and for the species previously published the synonymy alone is given, for which reasons it is impossible to prove that his determinations are unquestionable. It is to be acknowledged as a fact of value, that Mr. Ch. Girard first used in his descriptions the specifically different shape of the first pair of abdominal legs in the male, and the different breadth of the dorsal area.

He has divided the species into three groups, with the following characteristics: I. Rostrum subquadrangularly elongated, terminated anteriorly by three conical and acute spines, the two lateral smaller than the middle one, which forms the tip. Extremity of the anterior pair of abdominal legs in the male straight and acute. (7 spec.) II. Rostrum generally broad, conical, and short, with margins entire and toothless, terminated anteriorly by an acute and comparatively short point. Anterior pair of abdominal legs in the male recurved at their extremity, the tip of which is rounded. (9 spec.) III. Rostrum very much elongated, conical, tapering, provided on both sides and rather near the extremity with a small and acute spine, sometimes, however, but very slightly developed. (4 spec.)

Concerning the species described by Mr. Ch. Girard, — I have given my opinion at some length in my descriptions, — I may here make the following remarks: *C. Pealei* I consider as a full-grown *C. affinis; C. montanus, Diogenes,* and *pusillus* I am not able to separate from *C. Bartonii;* and *C. longulus* is possibly an abnormal specimen of the same species. *C. Blandingii* is not the species described by Harlan, but is *C. troglodytes,* Le Conte. *C. acutissimus* is the second form of the male of *C. acutus.* Some of my determinations may be incorrect; I hope hereafter to be able to compare the typical specimens preserved in the collection of the Smithsonian Institution.

The description and the detailed account of the burrowing habits of *C. Diogenes* given by Mr. Ch. Girard are very interesting, and, so far as I know, they are still the most complete description of this peculiar manner of living. Besides the remarks by Mr. John D. Godman, which I have not seen, Professor Erichson has mentioned the burrowing habits of some Australian species, and in the last edition of Cuvier's "Regnè Animal," the burrowing habits of an American species which severely damages the rice-fields of the Southern States are quoted from a communication by Dr. John Le Conte.

1855. Dr. John Le Conte has given, in the Proc. Acad. Phila., VII. 400, "Descriptions of new Species of *Astacus* from Georgia." Of the species described by Mr. Ch. Girard all but one are from the South, the others are from the Northern, and mostly from the Eastern States. Therefore Dr. John Le Conte's monograph is far more interesting. He describes nine species from Georgia, eight new; and there are two more, only seen by him. He remarks that he has preferred the old generic name *Astacus,* because the very slight and not very apparent differences which has been adopted to distinguish these two genera appear to him of little moment. Their color, says Dr. John Le Conte, is generally lost with their life, so that it is of little value in the description. "All that I have ever seen were much of the same color, — a reddish brown, inclining to dark olive." I do not find that any marks can be definitely pointed out by which we can distinguish those which are subterranean from those which are aquatic. It is possible to determine the species by the elaborate descriptions, especially by the shape of the rostrum and the hands, and the breadth of the areola. The types of six species, contained in the Museum of the Philadelphia Academy, have been kindly communicated to me by Professor Leidy, viz. *A. troglodytes, spiculifer, fossarum, angustatus, latimanus, advena.*

Concerning his species, I would remark that *A. troglodytes* is synonymous with *C. Blandingii* Girard, and that from this species I am not able to separate *A. fossarum*. But having seen only one female type, the identity must be proved by further investigation. *A. Blandingii* Le Conte is identical with *C. Lecontei* Hagen, or perhaps with Harlan's species. *A. spiculifer* is without doubt a new and good species, but I am not able to separate it decisively from the type *A. angustatus*. *A. latimanus* and *advena* are new species; *A. maniculatus* is entirely unknown to me.

After these reductions, we find the number of different species in the United States to be twenty, — fifteen given by Mr. Ch. Girard and five by Dr. John Le Conte.

1852. Professor James D. Dana, in his Synopsis Familiarum Crustaceorum, in the Proc. Acad. Phila., VI. 15, divided the old genus *Astacus* into two genera, *Astacoides* (segmentum abdominis maris primum appendicibus carens) and *Astacus* (segmentum abdominis maris primum appendicibus instructum). With *Astacoides* are united *Engœus* and *Cheraps*, with *Astacus Cambarus*. He describes (p. 20) *Astacus leniusculus* from the Columbia River "pedesquinti branchias parvas gerentes." In his celebrated work, United States Expl. Exped., Crustacea, I. 522, he says: "Among the distinctions subdividing the genus *Astacus*, that of the presence or absence of prehensile appendages to the first abdominal segments in males, fitted for use in coition, appears to be of the first importance. But the texture of the caudal segment, whether calcareous or not to its tip, cannot be of much value in classification, for it varies in the same species with age, and must therefore be somewhat dependent on the size of the species. The presence of a branchia to the posterior pair of legs may prove to be a characteristic of importance, requiring a subdivision accordingly; but of this we doubt. In the American species without this branchia, which the author has examined, the medial posterodorsal region of the carapax is narrow linear, while in the European species and that from Oregon, having the full number of branchiæ, this region is quite broad. But we cannot say how far this is generally true. For the reasons stated, we accept of *Astacoides* as a distinct genus, separated from *Astacus* by the absence of appendages from the first segment of the abdomen, and we unite with it *Cheraps* and *Engœus* of Erichson. The occurrence of the *Engœi* in holes in moist earth is not peculiar to that group, for the same habit has been observed by Professor S. F. Baird in an American species. *Cheraps* may perhaps be retained as a subgenus under *Astacoides*, on account of the absence of the posterior branchiæ; and, on the same ground, and no other of importance, *Cambarus* may be retained as a subgenus under *Astacus*." For this reason the author has retained *Cambarus* as a subgenus under *Astacus*, in his Synopsis, I. 523, and in the revision and emendation, II. 1433.

Astacus leniusculus is described, p. 524, and figured, pl. 33, fig. 1. I have never seen this species. *Astacus Bartonii*, locality uncertain, possibly from Brazil, is described, p. 525, and figured, pl. 33, fig. 2. The figure differs from all *C. Bartonii* which I have seen, even from the types communicated by Professor Stimpson and Professor Leidy. The rostrum, the antennal lamina, the areola, and the hand are so different in shape that evidently there must be a mistake. The patria, "possibly from Brazil," is another stumbling-block. In the Museum of the Philadelphia Academy are two Astaci labelled Potamobius spec. West Indies, and one labelled Bahia. But all three are undoubtedly the European *Astacus fluviatilis*. Perhaps the labels have been changed. Another small specimen, labelled Brazil, agrees in the shape of the rostrum with the figure given by Dana, but this curious species is neither an *Astacus* nor a *Cambarus*, but perhaps a *Cheraps*. It is a male, without the first pair of abdominal legs. Astacidæ must be very rare in Brazil, as it was impossible for Professor Agassiz and the members of the Thayer Expedition to obtain any specimen, or even to ascertain the existence of any *Astacus* species, in the vast country investigated by them. It must be remarked that Erichson has never seen the *Astacus Chilensis* mentioned by him; perhaps it is not a *Cambarus* at all.

1857. Professor W. Stimpson, in "The Crustacea and Echinodermata of the Pacific Shores of North America," Journ. Boston Soc. N. H., VI. (and separate, Cambridge, 1857 - 58, p. 93, pl. 6), gives detailed descriptions of three new species, — *A. nigrescens*, from San Francisco; *A. Trowbridgii*, from Astoria, and *A. Klamathensis*, from the Klamath Lake. Also shorter notices of *A. Gambelii*, *A. leniusculus*, and *A. Oreganus*. He has kindly communicated to me the types of the new species. They are apparently a very valuable addition to the North American fauna, as is also the negative fact that as yet not a single species of *Cambarus* has been found in the States of the Pacific shores.

1866. Spence C. Bate, in "Vancouver Island Crabs," in the Naturalist in Vancouver's Island and British Columbia, by J. Keast Lord, London, II. 278, says that *A. Klamathensis* is to be found in all streams east of the Cascades.

1864. Mr. H. Lucas has given a Note on *Astacus pellucidus*, which I have not seen, in the Bullet. Soc. Entom. Paris, p. iv.

1857. Mr. H. de Saussure, in Geneva, describes in his "Note carcinologique zur la famille des Thalassides et sur celle des Astacides," Rev. et Magas. de Zoologie, IX. pp. 99 - 102 et 503, three new species of *Cambarus* from America, *C. consobrinus* from Cuba, *C. Montezumæ* and *C. Aztecus*, both from Mexico. The descriptions are too short for a certain judgment, especially as I have not seen any species from Cuba, and but one female from Mexico. It is impossible, from the descriptions alone, to separate *C. consobrinus* from *C. Cubensis*, and the two other species from *C. Mexicanus*.

1858. Mr. H. de Saussure, in Mém. de la Soc. Phys. de Genève, T. 14, Pars II., pp. 456–461, Tab. III. f. 21–23, gives detailed descriptions and figures of the three before-mentioned species. His remark, that the *Cambarus* prefer the marshes and muddy waters, is apparently not of general value. Many species of *Cambarus*, perhaps the greater part, live in pure running water; for some species it is directly stated by Dr. LeConte.

I find it impossible to separate the species described by Mr. De Saussure from the species described by Mr. Erichson, but a judgment from two descriptions (I have seen only one female) is always doubtful. I am not sure that the hooked legs described by Mr. De Saussure correspond with those of Mr. Erichson. I think Mr. De Saussure's second and third pairs of legs are the third and the fourth of Erichson, the latter commencing the numbering of the legs with the great claws, Mr. De Saussure beginning with the pair next after the great claws. I think the words in the Note by *C. Montezumæ*, "son *C. Mexicanus* en est bien distinct par le troisième article inerme de la *quatrieme* paire des pattes," is otherwise not intelligible. In *C. consobrinus* the second joint of the legs is said to be hooked; if this be not a typographic error, it is a strange exception.

C. consobrinus is not at all compared with *C. Cubensis* Erichs.; perhaps it is unknown to Mr. De Saussure. The two descriptions show no difference. The lamina of the antennæ, f. 21, b., has no apical external spine, — perhaps an error.

C. Montezumæ does not differ from *C. Mexicanus*, and *C. Aztecus* seems identical with *C. Wiegmanni*. But I confess that my materials are too imperfect to decide this question.

ON THE CONSTANCY OF THE SPECIFIC CHARACTERS AMONG ASTACIDÆ.

The examination of the constancy of the specific characters was a chief point in my labor, especially because Mr. Gerstfeldt, in his excellent monograph concerning the fresh-water Crustacea of Europe, has reduced the number of described species to only two, by proving that the characters relied on in their separation are far from being constant.

The exceedingly rich mass of material before me, thus far unrivalled for such a labor, has permitted a very extensive and careful examination of the constancy of the characters. Otherwise viewed, it could not be denied that this rich material — there being more than a hundred specimens of some species — would rather serve to obstruct the judgment of the worker.

Dr. J. Le Conte, in his careful monograph of the Astaci of Georgia, says: "The shape of the rostrum and of the chelæ and the size of the areola vertebralis affords the best characteristic marks. I have never known this last character to vary in any degree. In the two others there may occur slight differences of development, not, however, so great as to be of any moment." According to these remarks, Dr. J. Le Conte seems to be convinced that the size of the areola vertebralis is alone constant and always identical, and thus confirms the result of the labor undertaken some years afterward for the European species by Mr. Gerstfeldt. I have to add that Mr. Gerstfeldt does not speak at all of the areola vertebralis, because it is not so well marked in the true Astacus, and that Mr. Gerstfeldt also has proved all the other characters to be variable in some degree. I am obliged to go a little further, and to state that, according to my observations, even the areola vertebralis varies to a greater or less extent.

Abnormal Gigantic Specimens. — It is very necessary to give up the idea that specific characters should bear a mathematical identity. Crustacea, as is well known, grow continually, and possibly become very old. Therefore we sometimes find of a species, which commonly has certain and smaller dimensions, some old and gigantic individuals, differing in many characters (viz. in sculpture, armature, relative size of parts and members) from the common examples of the same species. As progress is made in the cultivation of the land, and the improvement of the rivers, and especially as the population of the country increases, these giants become more and more rare in the species used as food, as in *A. fluviatilis* of Europe. Perhaps the extraordinary dimensions given by Rafinesque fifty years ago — for *A. limosus* nine inches, for *A. fossor* six inches, while at this time the specimens seen by me are only half as large — are explicable in this way. I remark, however, that the American species are not commonly used as food, except by the French population of the Southern States.

But even aside from these abnormal instances, other younger and older specimens present quite a variable material for comparison and description. If you state, for instance, that the specific characters should be only taken from the full-grown specimens, this statement is not at all decisive, because it is impossible to determine whether a specimen be full grown or not. In Norway it is against the law to sell lobsters not full grown; and the law considers every lobster over eight inches long as full grown, because it is supposed to have spawned three times. But the lobster may become twice that size; it would then differ in sculpture, armature, and the relative size of its members, as mentioned before. The real difference is far greater, as it is reasonable to consider every lobster after its first spawn, although then much smaller, as a full-grown animal.

Although a good and complete description of a species should enable us to determine both the young and the full-grown specimens, still the careful and right choice of the specific characters seems to depend largely upon the taste of the describer and upon the richness of the materials at his command.

Accidental Variations. — In the first place, all accidental variations are to be excluded. Crustacea are known very easily to reproduce parts damaged or accidentally lost; but these regenerated parts do not often reach the size or form of the old portions. Of course I do not here speak of variations, which are very easy to be recognized, as when one or more limbs are reproduced on one side. But I have seen specimens with the same limbs renewed on both sides, and such specimens, especially if one do not have before him more examples, are sometimes very difficult to recognize, and they often occasion errors (cf. *A. Gambelii*). The most prominent parts of the Crustacea are easily damaged and reproduced, as the claws, the antennæ and their basal lamina, the rostrum, and the caudal lamellæ. But sometimes the more protected parts are found affected in the same manner, as the first pair of abdominal legs, and even the epistoma.

Differences of Age. — The differences of age are of vast importance, and have a great influence on the right understanding of any species. The very young and newly hatched animals are, without doubt, recognizable by anybody. Afterward, as stated, there is more difficulty. The rich materials of the Museum allow the following remarks: —

Though generally the body has a constant form, I agree with Mr. Gerstfeldt, that even here there is no mathematical identity. The oval shape of the body, its greater or less convexity, its compression or depression, the abrupt or gradual curving of its sides, are somewhat variable. These variations, it is true, do not exceed certain limits; but they are here more troublesome, as in the great number of species they seem sufficient to obliterate the specific characters. I say expressly "seem sufficient," as the greatest difficulty consists in expressing these differences clearly and definitely by words, while the worker, who sees the species before him, separates them more easily.

Differences in the Shape of the Head. — A more essential difference in the shape of the head and the great claws is to be found in specimens of different ages. Here these differences are more striking and more troublesome than the relations of the different parts. Their length and breadth, their thickness, compared with that of the body and its limbs, undergo marked fluctuations, and these fluctuations are far from being of the same kind in all the groups of our fresh-water Crustacea. In the several species of the group, of which *Cambarus acutus* is the type, the young animals always have a three-toothed rostrum, though in the older individuals the lateral teeth are often nearly or entirely obliterated. In the group of *Cambarus Bartonii*, on the contrary, the younger animals do not differ in the shape of the rostrum from the older, although the limbs of the claw-legs are in their proportions sometimes very different in older individuals, the brachium longer even comparatively, the claw longer and thicker, the fingers more curved and furthermore separated from each other at the bases, while other similar differences are to be seen in the antennæ and their appendages, in the shape of the rostrum, and the front margin of the cephalothorax.

Differences in Sculpture. — The differences in the sculpture and armature are naturally much more considerable. The punctation, the granulation, the flat scales, the thorns, the spines, and the teeth, the margins of the thorax and of the great claws, are little or not at all developed in the younger specimens; they are a little more visible in the middle-aged animals; even those that are old and full grown sometimes differ considerably in the degree of development.

Hairyness. — On the contrary, the hairyness of some parts seems a constant character for species, even in the younger animals. But this character is to be found only in few species, and is not generally important.

Older Specimens. — On the whole, it may be said that in the older Astacidæ the form and the sculpture are more strongly exarated; the claw of the first legs is larger and heavier. But, besides the dimorphism of the males described further on, individuals are to be found in a so-called retrograde or arrested development.

Retrograde Development. — Older and larger animals are found, which in the degree of sculpture and armature are considerably behind specimens of similar or even smaller size, and these have apparently stopped at a lower stage of development. Naturally, these individuals are to be found mostly in the group in which the development of the sculpture and of the great claws is greatest, as in the group of *Cambarus acutus.*

Postabdomen. — The form of the postabdomen is constant in the different species; in the females it is usually broader. The external angles of the postabdominal segments are differently shaped, more or less rounded or acuminated. These differences are specific and constant, but usually they are not very remarkable, and they are difficult to describe. The "lamina analis," especially the middle lamina, offers specific characters. Its basal part always has two or three teeth on each side of its front margin. But I must remark, that in shape and size, and even in number, the teeth are often variable. Nevertheless, when rich materials are at hand this character is useful. The form and especially the margin of the apical part of the middle lamina are likewise in some species different, and in some degree constant. I remark, as an example of the difficulty of recognizing occasional accidental variations, that I have seen of *Astacus Gambelii* but two males, one with the apical margin of the middle lamina exactly rounded, the other exactly notched. I consider the latter as perhaps accidentally altered.

Hands.—The hands, or great claws, are, in every description, carefully used as one of the best specific characters. No doubt their form and sculpture are quite different in many species, and offer characters most easy of recognition. Nevertheless, these characters become more and more uncertain as the materials in hand are richer. As I have stated before, the development, the size, and the sculpture of the hands vary considerably between the first and second form males and the females, between the young, middle-aged, full-grown, and gigantic specimens. Even the relative length and breadth differ; the brachium surpasses the eyes or not; the fingers are equal or unequal in length, longer than the rest of the hand or not, straight or curved, denticulated at the margins or not; the carpus has the spines more or less numerous, more or less developed. In the full-grown specimens the hands are surely a constant and good specific character, but even here they vary to a certain degree, and finally it is not at all easy, with scanty materials, to determine with certainty whether a specimen be full grown or not. Therefore I have never given in the different species the exact and detailed measurements of these parts, which are noted by some authors, as I have found these measurements of very little value. The measurements given by me are average measurements, generally of the most full-grown specimens. But I have always been careful to record all the different forms of the hands which I have observed in each species.

The hairyness of the hands, which, like a beard, a brush, or a pencil, is found in some species (*A. Gambelii*, *C. penicillatus immunis*, etc.), seems constant and a very good specific character; the same is true of the partial hairyness on the first pair of maxillary legs (outside and below, or outside only).

On the basal joint of the fourth and of the fifth pair of legs there occurs a little knob (capitulum), differing in its shape in given species in a constant manner.

Colors.—The colors are apparently of no value. I have not seen living specimens, but Dr. John Le Conte says directly: "All that I have ever seen were much of the same color," and "their color is generally lost with their life, so that it is of little value in the description." All the alcoholic specimens have a similar color,—reddish brown, inclining to a more or less dark olive or dirty yellow. In certain species red spots are occasionally to be found in some species, as noticed in my descriptions. I should remark that the color is apparently altered in alcohol as time advances. The specimens of *C. Bartonii* received within a few weeks are reddish brown, the older ones nearly yellow.

Dr. John Le Conte says expressly that the burrowing species do not differ from those that are aquatic.

THE SEXUAL PECULIARITIES OF THE ASTACIDÆ.

The sexual differences, aside from the genital parts, are often very considerable. In the female the great claw is shorter, smaller, and not so well developed. The sculpture and armature are less, the postabdomen mostly broader, and its legs stronger. Apparently the females have, in many parts, retained the characters of the younger animals. But sometimes there are females with a development not at all inferior, or with one even superior, to that of the males. I am not certain whether, as in the males, any dimorphism is to be found.

Abnormal Females.—It is not impossible in this way to explain, and thus indeed may be explained, many apparent anomalies in females. In these females we find a tendency to a more masculine development, as in the aforesaid males a tendency to a feminine development. Nevertheless, even the rich materials of some species now in my hands are not rich enough to enable me to solve by anatomical examination this interesting question.

The Abdominal Legs of the Males.—The sexual parts of the Astacidæ, especially in the North American *Cambarus*, offer very good and constant specific characters. The abdominal legs of the Astacidæ possess a short, transverse, inwardly situated basal article, and a longer doubled flagellum, consisting of two approximated narrow bands of a more membraneous consistency, flexible, and sprinkled with hairs on the outside. In the males, the first and the second pair are partly transformed. The second pair has the basal half of the inner flagellum corneous and thickened, but the apical half retains the same membraneous shape as the external flagellum and the flagellum of all the following legs. The corneous basal half is dilated at the end and rolled from the inside outward, forming a channel. The first pair of abdominal legs is even more transformed. The articulation between the basal limb and the flagellum is gone, and also the whole external flagellum, as well as the membraneous apical part of the inner flagellum. The remains of the first abdominal leg form a corneous limb, with the apical half dilated and rolled from the outside inward, forming also a channel. This kind of shape is most easily understood in the true *Astacus* from Europe and from California. In the American species of *Cambarus* we find the modifications and different exarations forming, as stated before, very good specific characters. The dilated apical half is so closely rolled together that the channel no longer exists, except very superficially, and the closely rolled part is transformed into two approximate corneous solid cylinders, united above, while below there is an apparent suture, constituting the rest of the channel before described. The tip in each of the two cylinders is not simply truncated, as in the European and Californian *Astacus*, but transformed into more or less corneous hooks and teeth. We find also in *Cambarus* the tip oı the first abdominal legs bifid, and the two branches more or less elongated, equal or not in length and breadth, straight or curved, and very well adapted to form specific characters. Having examined a very great number of specimens, I am able to state that these different forms are very constant in the same species. Naturally here, as elsewhere throughout the group, it is not possible to find an exact mathematical identity, but a constancy within certain limits, and I was able to observe and figure some variations.

The rolled part of the second pair of abdominal legs — I have remarked before that it is rolled in the opposite direction — is apparently analogous to this formation in the first pair, and is formed in the European species exactly in the same manner as in the first abdominal legs. In the *Cambarus* the apical end of the dilated plate is considerably more rolled than the basal end, assuming in this manner a triangular shape. It is interesting to find the same arrangement in the true American *Astacus*.

The Purpose of this Structure. — The purpose of this structure of the first two pairs of abdominal legs is easily explained. The seminal fluid coming out of the basal part of the fifth legs by an open circular aperture, must be conveyed to the sexual aperture of the female, situated farther forward in the inner basal part of the third legs. The first pair of the abdominal legs of the male, being situated closer to the venter, is very well adapted by its channelled shape (represented in the *Cambarus* by the shallow suture) to direct the seminal fluid to the designed part in the female. It is likewise well to notice that the transformed shape of the second abdominal legs gives a considerable help for this purpose in two ways. First, the dilated part, especially in the *Cambarus*, is well adapted to be inserted into the sutured part of the first legs, and mechanically to support the first legs in a horizontal position. The rolled part also serves to complete the channel made by the first legs for the direction of the seminal fluid, and it is well to remark that the inverse manner of rolling, as before stated, serves more completely to prevent any of the ejected seminal fluid from taking a wrong direction. In the Madagascar and most of the Australian Astacidæ these modified abdominal legs, fitted for use in coition, are entirely wanting, and the conveyance of the seminal fluid is perhaps more simple and imperfect.

The Females. — Regularly in the articulated animals, especially in the insects, we find in the genera or families in which the organization of the sexual parts differs specifically in the males, that the females also exhibit differences more or less adapted to the male organs. The striking differences in the male organs of the *Cambari* made the presence of analogous differences in the females probable. But these are not to be found. The female sexual aperture is always oval, closed by a thick membraneous plate, firmly attached by the outside half, moving and opening inwardly. The oviduct is a simple hole, and, as far as I know, there are no specific differences. In a new gigantic Australian species of *Astacoides*, very near *A. nobilis* Dana the female aperture is more elongated and surrounded by a circular barbe of hairs, apparently designed for the better conveyance of the seminal fluid in a species without first abdominal first legs.

The manner of coition of the Astacidæ has been as yet rarely observed (Cuvier Règne anim., T. IV. p. 89, says: "L'accouplement s'opère ventre contre ventre"); but, on comparing closely the situation of the sexual parts of the male, it is evident that the first abdominal legs partly enter into the oviduct, and certainly no more than with their corneous tips. The length and situation of the parts, and the circumstance that the second pair of legs is apparently firmly fitted in coition to the first legs so as to prevent a farther entrance, seems to prove that perhaps this arrangement only serves to open the membraneous plate of the female parts at the right time. In all the species of *Cambarus* the part of the first abdominal legs of the male, which may and which can only enter into the female aperture, is well marked and separated by a transverse superficial suture.

It is well known that the females of the Astacidæ possess no receptaculum seminis, and so the introduction of the seminal fluid seems without purpose. But as it is stated by Milne-Edwards that he once discovered spermatophores in the female aperture of *Carcinus*, which also has no receptaculum seminis, perhaps the same may occur in the Astacidæ.

Annulus Ventralis.—The female sexual aperture offers no specific characters, but we find some in the ventral, or rather sternal, plates between the last two pairs of thoracic legs, especially between those of the fourth pair. These differences not being very remarkable in the true *Astacus*, although they exist, I never find them mentioned by the authors. But the American *Cambarus* shows well-defined characters, although difficult to describe.

Between the fourth legs we find a broad trapezoidal plate, more or less excavated and elongated in the different species. The posterior end of this plate is ordinarily dilated and on every side angularly protracted. Its surface is smooth or tuberculated. Behind this plate is a supernumerary corneous organ (repeated even between the fifth legs), which gives specific characters. This organ—named annulus in my descriptions—generally forms a short cone, with a transverse oval base and a depressed tip. This cone is divided in the medial line of the body by a denticulated suture, with inflated margins. The tip is often more or less depressed, or even impressed, forming a deep, transverse hole, crossing the denticulated suture. Tab. II. f. 126.

We find inside two approximated, inflated, or vermiform ridges, following exactly the outside suture. The size of this corneous cone, and the shape of the suture and apical hole, differ considerably in the different species, and seem, to some extent, constant in the same species. The structure and shape of this organ seem to be for some sexual purpose. The ridges (in *C. acutus, Clarkii, Bartonii*, etc.) have an inner open entrance on the front margin, and seem opened between the suture outside on the hind margin. In the annulus I found fat and fibrous matter imbedded, and perhaps a glandular mass, which it was not easy to determine in the old alcoholic specimens. Nevertheless, the whole apparatus seems to be fitted for some secretion. Tab. II. f. 127.

The corneous cone in the species of *Cambarus* is well separated from the ventral plate, being only united to it by a membrane, movable in the young and sometimes even in the full-grown individuals. This is a specific character (*C. troglodytes*).

In the true *Astacus* this organ exists; still it is not separated from the ventral plate, except by an external channelled space; it forms a slender transverse ridge, varying in shape in different species, but not so conspicuously, and having no denticulated suture or secretional apparatus.

I have sometimes thought that this apparatus might perhaps serve for gluing the eggs to the abdominal legs; but as this does not exist in the true *Astacus*, it seems improbable. By what is possibly a singular coincidence, I have failed to find, among specimens from more than thirty localities and among several hundred females of all sizes, a single female, in the *Cambari* of the group *C. acutus*, with the eggs attached. Two females have young between the abdominal legs, but no remains of the egg-cases. Do the females of the group of *C. acutus* lay their eggs in a manner different from the other *Cambari?* I presume not.

Eggs: their Attachment and Bursting.—The eggs in the Astacidæ are always attached, as in some insects (in *Chrysopa, Hemerobius, Mantispa*), by a short stem. Before the appearance of the egg the glue is excreted from the female sexual aperture, fixed, and drawn out into a stem; finally the egg is fixed upon it. It is also to be presumed that the Astacidæ fix their eggs in the same manner. I should remark that the stem in the *Astaci* is always much stronger than in the *Cambari.*

It is, perhaps, interesting to notice that the eggs in the true Astacidæ are always burst in the same manner, viz. into two parts perpendicularly, the segments remaining attached to the stem. This condition makes its probable that the *Astacus* embryo has a particular egg-burster similar to that in the insects, although these interesting parts are little observed or known even by entomologists.

Development of the First Pair of Abdominal Legs in the Male.—It is easy to discriminate between the sexes of very young individuals of *Cambarus Clarkii.* This is the case with those only 0.3 inch long, and while they still occupy the postabdomen of the mother. In the females the sexual aperture is visible at the base of the third set of legs. The first abdominal segment is without any appearance of abdominal legs; in all the other segments the abdominal legs are well developed, their length being nearly two thirds of the breadth of the postabdomen, the basal article being oblong, while the length of the doubled flagellum is a little greater.

In the males the first segment has on each side a little knob, somewhat longer than broad, turning inward. In the interior the developing leg is visible, and its articulation seems marked. This oval knob, with rounded tip, is the beginning of the first pair of abdominal legs. I have seen the same form of the first abdominal legs in the young of *C. Bartonii*, even 0.55 inches long. Tab. II. Figs. 133, 134.

Second Form of the Males.—I have examined the further development in *Cambarus acutus*. In the younger specimens, 1.7 inch long, the legs are more developed, the basal third articulated. The shape of the legs is nearly the same as in the full-grown animal, but narrower, more curved, the tip a little broader, the teeth more obtuse. In the older specimens, 2.7 inches long, the legs are the same as in the full-grown animal, which is over four inches long. Occasionally, both in younger and in full-grown specimens, the articulation is partly gone, but its remains are still visible on the upper margin; in some cases the articulation has entirely disappeared.

This form, which is always visible in the very young and in middle-aged specimens, ordinarily with an articulation, I have described as the second form of the male.

First Form of the Males.—In all species seen and examined by me, many old, full-grown males have the first pair of legs of a particular shape, analogous in a certain view to the form before described, and always found in the young animals, but differing in the following particulars.

The articulation is entirely gone; the tip of the leg is more distinctly finished and not so membraneous; the hooks are horny; the teeth or bifid ends longer and more separated; the hairyness, if any exists, more profuse. I have figured these parts in nearly all the species, and described them as the first form of the male. I think it is well to observe that, in the second form of the males, they are always developed in a manner visibly less complete than in the first form.

The males of the second form differ also in another way from those of the first form. The hooks on the third article of the third, or in some groups of the third and of the fourth, pair of legs are smaller and less developed. The whole body has less size and width, the sculpture is not so well finished, while the claws are shorter, narrower, and more like those of the female.

A closer examination of the rich materials at the Museum shows that all the young male specimens of *Cambarus*, without exception, pertain to the second form. But there are also not a few large males belonging to the second form, which have retained the articulation and the shape of the tip of the first abdominal legs proper to the young specimens. The articulation is sometimes entirely or partially gone. Among nearly fifty full-grown males of *Cambarus acutus*, about twenty-five belong to the second form; while among fifty young males, nearly a dozen have, for the most part or entirely, lost the articulation. Tab. II. Figs. 112, 113.

The discovery that every species of *Cambarus* possesses two different forms of males was made by Professor L. Agassiz,* and kindly communicated to me.

Dimorphorism, or perhaps a Sterile Form.— The existence of a second form of the male, if it were no more than a passage or metamorphotic form, would not be extraordinary. But the great number of full-grown second-form specimens in every species, which are often even larger than the first-form males, seems to prove that they are individuals which have remained in a sexual stage that does not agree with their corporal development, — in short, that they are perhaps sterile.

The objection that these second-form males may be individuals shortly before or shortly after the casting of the skin I can surely refute, as I have seen many specimens at this stage of growth; the Museum collections exhibiting the animal in all the different phases of its existence.

Another objection, that the males of the second form, or perhaps those of the first form, are abnormally developed individuals, is refuted by the great number of the two forms existing and living together.

The conjecture, on the other hand, that the second-form males may be sterile, is really supported by the anatomical examination of the two forms in the principal groups of *Cambarus*.

Internal Sexual Parts of Cambarus Male. Of C. acutus. Tab. II. Figs. 120 - 123.— In two full-grown males of *Cambarus acutus*, first and second form, both four inches long, the testicles are trilolate, as in *Astacus fluviatilis*, but much smaller, the vasa deferentia shorter. In the first-form males the two superior lobes are pyriform, truncated above, united below in a membraneous hole a little shorter than the testicles, and connected with the third inferior lobe. Where the two superior are united, the vas deferens begins on each side, being vermiform and shorter than the body. The testicles in a *Cambarus acutus*, four inches in length, are but 0.3 inch long; while in an *Astacus fluviatilis*, two inches in length, they are 0.6 inch long, thus much larger,

* Intending many years ago to describe the North American Astacidæ, he made a close inspection of the material he had collected for that purpose. Observing the different shape and organization of the first pair of abdominal legs, he was led to this important discovery.

and there is no membraneous hole, as the three lobes are closely approximated; the vasa deferentia are also stronger, more curved, and have greater length than the body. Their end is visibly more dilated than in *Cambarus acutus.*

In the second-form male of *Cambarus acutus* the testicles are similar but smaller, the superior lobes narrower, oval; the inferior lobe is acuminated, narrower, and not bigger than the connecting hole of the superior lobes. The vasa deferentia are shorter. The microscopic examination of the contents of the testicles offers no further argument, as the specimens have remained too long in alcohol.

Of C. virilis. Tab. II. Figs. 128–132.—In the first-form male of *Cambarus virilis,* 3.2 inch long, the testicles are somewhat similar, but longer, being in length 0.7 inch. The superior lobes have a prismatic form, with diverging acuminated ends. The prismatic part is excavated above, and much separated from the smaller and compressed hole. The inferior lobe is long and compressed, seen sidewise, oval, and truncated behind. The vasa deferentia are longer than in *Cambarus acutus,* while their ends are not visibly dilated.

In the second form of *Cambarus virilis,* 2 inches long, the testicles are shorter, the superior lobes prismatic, but the superior part is not much separated; the inferior lobe is shorter, beginning with a narrow hole, laterally more compressed; the vasa deferentia are shorter and narrower.

Of C. Bartonii. Tab. II. Figs. 135–138.—In the first form of the third principal group in *Cambarus Bartonii,* 2 inches long, the sexual parts are more similar to those of *Astacus fluviatilis.* They are 3.5 inches long, the superior lobes oval and large, while their superior tip is a little contracted. Connected by an inferior, well-separated, smaller membraneous hole with the equally long hole of the inferior lobe, there is to be found behind the connecting joint an inflated tubercle, while lower down there is another which is similar but smaller. The inferior lobe is pyriform, inflated behind, somewhat compressed laterally. The vasa deferentia are stronger and longer, the ends being visibly dilated.

In the second-form male of *Cambarus Bartonii,* 2 inches long, the testicles are shorter, the superior lobes more trigonal, the inferior narrower, elongated, much more compressed, acuminated behind, the connecting holes not so well separated and finished, without tubercles behind, while the vasa deferentia are narrower and shorter, the ends not being visibly dilated.

I may remark, that in the first-form males of *Cambarus acutus* and *Bartonii* the three lobes of the testicles exhibit the same granulated contents as in *Astacus fluviatilis.* But in *Cambarus virilis* they are white and have a fatty appearance, similar to those always found in the second-form males.

The sexual parts of the second-form males are so much less developed that it would be allowable to consider them as sterile. An anatomical examination of the second-form males without articulation in the first abdominal legs was not possible, as the materials were not sufficiently abundant.

As before stated, I surmise the presence of similar sterile females; which as viragoes show more of a male type.

An anatomical examination of the females of *Cambarus acutus* and *Bartoni* reveals some difference in the shape of the ovarium.

Internal Sexual Parts of the Cambarus Female. Of C. acutus. Table II. Fig. 123.—In *Cambarus acutus* the ovarium is nearly an inch in length, elongated, narrow. The two superior lobes are shorter, cylindrical, a little inflated at the base; the inferior lobe is elongated, conical. The connecting part is more enlarged, and gives on each side a large oviduct. Above this part is situated a strong membrane, which passes with an acuminated tip between the superior lobes; it is provided laterally with some bands of "musculi alati," while the fibres are strongly striated transversely. This membrane also shows several nerves, apparently belonging to the nervus sympathicus.

Of C. Bartoni. Table II. Fig. 129.—In *Cambarus Bartoni*, 2 inches in length, the ovarium is 0.65 inch long, and larger. The superior lobes are shorter and oval; the inferior a large cone. The oviduct is even broader. The membrane is similar to that in *Cambarus acutus*. In both species examined, the ovarium was filled with eggs of different sizes and degrees of development.

No Dimorphism in the true Astaci.—The existence of two forms of males in the *Cambarus* of North America has been proved by me in all species in which I was able to examine a large number of specimens. In five species, represented only by single specimens of first-form males or females, I have not seen the second form. But the existence of this second form will be by far the more interesting, since it seems that in the *Astacidæ* only the *Cambarus* possesses two forms of the male. I have examined nearly two hundred specimens of *Astacus fluviatilis* from different European localities (Germany, Switzerland, France, Scotland), without finding a difference in the males. I must add that I have not seen very young specimens, and do not know at all whether the young have the first pair of abdominal legs articulated as in the *Cambarus*. The smallest specimen seen by me is 1.5 inch long. Of the Californian *Astaci* I have not seen more than a dozen males. All these were quite full grown, and without any differences answering to the second form of *Cambarus*. Of the Amur species I have seen but one female.

Dimorphism in other Crustacea.—Perhaps this fact of the existence in the crustacea of two forms, one always sterile, is not unique. In the genera Lupa and Callinectes there are not rarely females with a very narrow and acute postabdomen. These it is very easy to separate from the ordinary females, with large and circular postabdomen. Professor L. Agassiz informs me that he has satisfied himself, by an anatomical examination of living specimens, that these females are sterile. I have found similar females with a narrower triangular abdomen in some other genera of *Brachyura.*

I am indebted to Mr. Alexander Agassiz for the information that F. Müller, Fuer Darwin, 1864, has described two forms of the male in *Orchestia Darwinii* and in *Tanais dubius.* He remarks that when found upon the shore the form of the second pair of gnathopoda varies from that of specimens found at a distance inland, where it lives under mouldy leaves in loose earth. In *O. Darwinii,* intermediate forms between the males with large and those with small hands are not to be detected, but in two other species, *O. tucurauna* and *O. tucuratinga,* the shape of the antennæ and of the hands changes even in the full-grown males.

The supposition that the first-form males only in *Cambarus* possess large hands for burrowing purposes is to be rejected, as the females also have the same burrowing habits.

The existence of two different forms of males in *Cambarus* is very important in the description of the species, and the fact that these forms are not recognized by all preceding authors may explain some erroneous determinations in their works.

Dimorphism in Insects.— The discovery of a dimorphism in the crustacea is all the more interesting, since as yet in the whole animal kingdom dimorphism was known only in the insects. There are many facts and communications scattered through entomological literature, of which a general review is very desirable. An anatomical examination of these dimorphic forms is still wanting, only the external differences having been thus far marked.

The dimorphism seems to be represented in two different ways; a difference only in the colors (dichroic forms of Brauer), or a difference in size and shape, and mostly in the female. I should remark that dimorphism, as observed in insects, occurs only in one sex of the same species, and mostly in the female. Perhaps in the ants and in the white ants — it seems more natural to range all the socially living insects, viz. the ants bees, wasps, and white ants under the same law — a dimorphism is to be found in both sexes.

Dimorphism consisting in different colors was long since observed, especially in Lepidoptera, in the hind wings of many Orthoptera, and in the females of Agrion. In the latter genus the well-known orange-colored females are probably sterile.

Dimorphism with difference in shape and size is also often observed. A very common case is the difference in the development of the wings.

The wings are either long and well developed, or short, or entirely wanting. The short-winged Orthoptera (Gryllus, Locusta, Blatta, Perla, Termes, Psocus) have been carefully described by Messrs. Fischer, Von Siebold, Lucas, Brauer, and myself; the short-winged or apterous Hemiptera, by Westwood and Uhler (Amphibiocorisiæ, Gerridæ, etc.); the short-winged Diptera by Schaum (*Ornithobia* and *Lipoptera*). Mr. Brauer has recently given an interesting paper upon dimorphism in the genus Neurothemis, which belongs to the Odonata. The dimorphic females have wings with a less complicated neuration and different colors. There is even a case of trimorphism in some butterflies, according to the observations of Mr. Wallace. *Papilio Ormenus*, from Celebes, has three distinct forms of females, and in some cases the number of female forms appears to be four. Dimorphism consisting in different shape and size is observed in the Lepidoptera (Equites, etc.), in the Coleoptera, in the Lamellicornia, and in the Longicornia, and perhaps in the Lymexylon and Hylecœtus; in the Hymenoptera (Cynips); in the Diptera (Phasia). The dimorphism in the Dipterous genus Phasia, discovered by Loew, is very remarkable. Having seen his specimens, I may be permitted to add here a written communication by Mr. Loew, sent to me some years ago and still unpublished: "In the genus Phasia every species has two male forms; one similar to the female, and another much larger, with the wings broader and more colored, and usually the body more colored. The two forms fly at the same time and unite with the same form of females. The genital parts of the larger males are in shape and size identical with those of the smaller males. There exist some intermediate forms of males, and it is sometimes, in certain species, possible to form a complete series, which seems to unite the two different forms. I say seems, because I have never seen a male which I hesitated to place in one of the two forms."

I have noticed here the occurrence of dimorphism in the insects to show how variable in the different families and genera is the mode of dimorphism, even from that observed in the *Astacidæ*. Perhaps a closer examination will disclose even some difference in the sexual parts in certain dimorphic insects, and it now seems probable that some forms, heretofore described as distinct species, will be hereafter recognized as only dimorphic variations. Still, it is possible that very different facts are to-day united under the same name of dimorphism.

Certainly the discovery of a dimorphism in another part of the Articulata, viz. in the Crustacea, leads us to suppose that it will be found also among the worms.

The Rarity of Varieties is an Important Character for Cambarus. — The rarity of varieties in the genus *Cambarus* is worthy of remark, and may be considered as an important character of this genus. In the true *Astacus*, the two species living in Europe vary so much that even by eminent naturalists these varieties have been taken for nine different species. In the genus *Cambarus*, the thirty-two known species show comparatively very few varieties. But of three of these, viz. *C. acutus*, *C. virilis*, and *C. Bartoni*, the described varieties differ in a more considerable manner; while perhaps some of them, especially of *C. Bartoni*, will be hereafter recognized as different species. Indeed, the fact is too striking to be overlooked; here there are few species and many varieties, there many species and few varieties.

CAMBARUS Erich.

The question, Is *Cambarus* a peculiar genus different from *Astacus* or not, is one of great importance to me as monographer. The historical statements already quoted are all that have been made, so far as I know, upon the subject. It would no doubt have been more easy for me to judge of the importance of the generic characters if I had been able to study in the same manner all the species of the old genus *Astacus*. But the materials before me, except for North America, are not sufficient; some genera are entirely unrepresented, of others only a few specimens are at my disposal. I therefore confess that my judgment upon a division of the old genus *Astacus* into more genera is not completed; still, after a rather close examination, I am convinced that *Cambarus* forms a very good and natural genus, and that, if it be not accepted, a very great part of the actually adopted genera must be equally rejected.

The differences between *Astacus* and *Cambarus* are as follow:—

1. The general form of *Astaci* is clumsier, coarser, and more oval. The *Cambari* are more elongated and more cylindrical.

2. The absence of the gill on the fifth pair of legs in *Cambarus* is first quoted by De Haan. *Cambarus* has seventeen, *Astacus* eighteen gills. But there is also another difference, not before noticed. In *Astacus* each pair of gills, except the single one on the fifth set of legs, has a broad, deeply folded membrane, closely fixed behind the most external gill lobe. In *Cambarus* this membrane is always wanting in the gills on the fourth pair of legs, but exists, as in *Astacus*, in all the others.

In the true *Astacus* all the gills with a folded membrane behind have a basal external bundle of shorter but broader and irregularly placed gill tubes; these are never to be found in *Cambarus*. The superior external plate of the fifth pair of legs in *Cambarus* is surrounded by longer featherlike hairs; in *Astacus* we find but few on the posterior border; *C. pellucidus* is similarly organized to the true *Astacus*.

I may remark that the breadth of the areola or the medial postdorsal region (Dana) seems not to depend, as it would be easy to suppose, upon the presence or absence of the gills on the fifth pair of legs. We find in some *Cambari* (*C. spiculifer, versutus*) this areola even as broad as in many true *Astaci* with gills (*A. Klamathensis, Gambeli*), but in general the areola is never so well marked in *Astacus* as in *Cambarus*.

3. The inner antennæ in *Astacus* have a peculiar structure and shape. They are always very short and more conical (the basis thicker); the inner flagellum is considerably more slender and shorter, while the joints of the flagellum are more spherical, calcareous, and more fragile. Of course the inner antennæ are easily broken in the preserved specimens. In *Cambarus* the inner antennæ are visibly longer, the flagellum is equally long, and of the same structure as the outer antennæ.

The lamina of the outer antennæ has a prismatic shape in *Astacus*, the external border is much thickened. In *Cambarus* the lamina is visibly more membranous.

The basal article of the inner antennæ has an anteapical spine beneath in *Astacus ;* in *Cambarus* this spine is always situated in the middle of the article, or more basally.

4. The epistoma in the true *Astacus* is more solid, conical, a little contracted before the tip. It is in *Cambarus* more flattened, often excavated beneath, always larger, and never contracted before the tip.

5. The ear, or what is considered the auditory organ, forms in *Cambarus* (as in *Astacoides, Homarus*, and perhaps in *Cheraps*) a very short cone or a slightly elevated ring, closed above by a membrane, considered as the tympanum. The true *Astaci* are an exception, and have this organ differently shaped, with a more elevated cone, rounded on the top, and a narrower tympanum behind.

6. The parts which serve for sexual purposes in *Cambarus* differ essentially from those in *Astacus*. In *Cambarus* these parts are organized in a particular manner, and differently in every species. This is very important, as it is well known that in the Articulata very nearly allied genera often differ constantly in such a manner. This difference seems a criterion for separating two genera in forms otherwise nearly related.

These differences are as follow: Dimorphism is to be found in the males. The first pair of abdominal legs is differently formed; the apical half is not simply rolled as in *Astacus*, but transformed into two solid approximated parts, with the tips more or less protracted and differently finished.

In the females is to be found behind the sternum, between the fourth (and fifth) pair of legs, a particular separated part, — annulus, — differently shaped in the different species. In *Astacus* this part exists indeed, but it is never separated from the sternum, and is represented by a ridge, either straight and transverse or curved and broken behind. The particular shape of the annulus in *Cambarus*, with its denticulated median suture and its transverse hollow impression, is evidently analogous to the form in *Astacus*, but produced in a different and exaggerated manner. The hinder part of the sternum is separated and curved, not backward, as in *Astacus*, but forward and entirely rolled.

I may remark that, according to my anatomical investigations into some species, the internal sexual parts in males and females of *Cambarus* differ from those in *Astacus*. The three lobes of the testicles and the ovarium are larger, rounded, and closely approximated in *Astacus*, the vasa deferentia longer than the body. In *Cambarus* the three lobes are small, elongated, and separated; the vasa deferentia shorter than the body.

It would be very interesting to prove that the young of the genus *Cambarus* are hatched from the eggs in a similar but more advanced stage of development than the young of the genus *Astacus*, described by Professor Rathke. But the materials in my hands are not sufficient for this purpose, the smallest seen by me being 0.3 inches long, and belonging to *C. Clarkii*. The rostrum is incurved, but always tridentate; the interior antennæ have the flagellum short, and the exterior branch visibly thicker than the interior. The three anterior pairs of legs have nearly the same shape, the first pair is a little longer. The appendage to the legs of the young lobster, described by Thompson, Rathke, and others, does not exist at all. The abdominal legs do exist. The hooks on the third and the fourth pair of legs of the males are not developed. It is easy, as I have before intimated, to discriminate between the two sexes. The eyes are visibly more developed than in the more advanced animals.

With reference to the further division of the genus *Cambarus*, it was especially important to decide whether all North American *Cambari* belonged to the same genus or to different genera. I am now convinced that all the species I have seen form only one genus, containing several more or less well-defined groups. In this manner the genera *Cambarus* and *Astacus* seem very natural and of equal value. But I have no doubt that some time the genus *Astacus* will be divided into three genera (for the European, North American, and Asiatic species), and *Cambarus* into three or it may be into six genera as Prof. Agassiz thinks.

The division of *Cambarus* into groups is not difficult, except in a certain view: first, as the most striking characters are to be found only in one sex, in the males; and secondly, as some species seem to form a sort of medium uniting the different groups. The first objection is only of value to the naturalist who works with few materials, perhaps mostly females, and is therefore not able to determine the groups to which his specimens belong. But here the fault lies only in the scantiness of his materials, and not in the principle of classification. The second objection would be more important if it were quite certain that there are intermediate species. Perhaps these species only seem to be intermediate, and if not, finally, Nature never agrees with the strict principles of a particular scheme, so that apparently capricious aberrations are to be found everywhere the stumbling-blocks of the naturalist who wishes to arrange everything in a regular series.

A principal character suggesting the division of *Cambarus* into groups is to be found in the hooked legs of the males. This character divides all the species into two great groups, one with hooks on the third and the fourth pair of legs, the other with hooks only on the third pair of legs. This characteristic seems preferable to the later mentioned one, because it unites forms which are related in all other respects, while the groups divided according to the form of the rostrum unite species which are otherwise quite unlike.

In number and situation the hooks are always identical and very sure. Among nearly a thousand males I have found only one abnormal male with no hooks at all. I have never observed any aberration in the group with hooks on the third and on the fourth pair of legs, except a few second-form males of *C. pellucidus*, with the hooks on the fourth legs very small, even in one case not at all developed. In the other group, with hooks on the third set of legs, sometimes, but very rarely, males are to be found with hooks more or less developed on the second pair of legs, but never on the fourth pair. I may add, that the second-form males always have less developed hooks, and that all show the hooks except the very young and newly hatched males.

It is worthy of remark, and seems to prove the importance of this character, that the hooks are situated on the same joint and at the same place as the embryonal appendages of the legs in the young lobsters (*Homarus*), described by Professor Rathke and others. These afterward disappear, and are not to be found at all in the young of *Astacus fluviatilis*. Indeed, these hooks do not exist in the young *Cambari*; their development is later; but the analogy is too striking to be overlooked, and suggests the great desirableness of an accurate acquaintance with the embryological development of *Cambarus*.

According to the number of hooked legs, *Cambarus* is also divided into two groups: —

I. Third and fourth legs hooked, — group of *C. acutus*.

II. Third legs hooked, — all the rest.

The second important character for the division of *Cambarus* into groups is the shape of the rostrum. Mr. Girard has employed this character as a principal one, and forms three groups, with the following characters: —

Rostrum subquadrangularly elongated, tridentated at the tip, — *C. affinis* and allied species.

Rostrum short, broad, conical, toothless, — *C. Bartoni* and allied species.

Rostrum very much elongated, conical, with a small and acute spine near the extremity, sometimes, however, but very slightly developed, — *C. acutus* and allied species.

This character is indeed good, but sometimes not so striking as to prevent a mistake, which even Mr. Girard himself made, in placing *C. pellucidus* in his first group. There are some species in every group, the exact place of which is uncertain. At first sight the *C. spiculifer* and *C. versutus* would be placed in the first group, and not in the third; *C. penicillatus* and *C. Wiegmanni* near *C. Bartoni* in the second group, and not in the third; *C. immunis* in the second, and not in the first; *C. advena* and *C. Carolinus* in the third, and not in the second, — to which in reality they respectively belong. But generally, I repeat, this character is good, if not *prima vista*, at least in connection with the other characters.

Nevertheless, in the rostrum is to be found another important charter. In one group the rostrum never has lateral teeth at the tip, in all others these lateral teeth are to be found, if not in the full-grown specimens, yet always in the young. But the latter fact renders this mark evidently less useful than the character taken from the hooked legs. In the last case only the newly hatched specimens have no hooks and are doubtful; but in the other instance only the newly hatched specimens always have teeth, while the full grown are sometimes toothless. *C. acutus* and the allied species always have in the young specimens well-developed teeth, and the form of the rostrum is therefore altered in such a manner as to place them *prima vista* in Mr. Girard's first group, near *C. affinis*. *C. penicillatus*, though toothless when full grown, has well-developed teeth when young. *C. immunis*, and in some degree *C. virilis*, *C. propinquus*, and others, are in the same condition.

According to the absence or presence of the lateral apical teeth of the rostrum, *Cambarus* is divided into two other groups, not coinciding with those already mentioned: —

I. Always toothless, — *C. Bartoni* and allied species.

II. With teeth, at least in the young, — all the rest.

Combining the two principal characters mentioned, — the number of the hooked legs and the toothless or toothed rostrum, — we find three well-defined groups: —

I. Third and fourth legs hooked, rostrum toothed, — *C. acutus* and allied species.

II. Third legs hooked, rostrum toothed, — *C. affinis* and allied species.

III. Third legs hooked, rostrum toothless, — *C. Bartoni* and allied species.

These groups coincide with those established by Mr. Girard, after removing his erroneously placed species, viz. *C. pellucidus*, *C. Oreganus*, *C. Gambeli*.

Some other characters serve to evince more or less clearly the naturalness of these groups.

The first abdominal legs of the males show three different forms: —

I. The exterior part is nearly truncated at the tip, with three little partly dilated corneous incurved teeth; the interior part has a short acute tip, for the most part outwardly directed, — *C. acutus* and allied species.

II. The two parts have elongated, straight, acute tips, — *C. affinis* and allied species.

III. The tips of the exterior part forms a larger tooth, which is strongly recurved; the tip of the interior part is broken, short, and conical, — *C. Bartoni* and allied species.

I may remark that there are three exceptions to this character: *C. extraneus*, belonging to the group of *C. affinis*, has the abdominal legs formed as in the group of *C. Bartoni; C. advena* and *C. Carolinus*, belonging to the group of *C. Bartoni*, have the abdominal legs similar to the group of *C. acutus*.

The other characters examined by me are not so striking. The antennæ are more slender, as long as, or longer than, the body in the group of *C. acutus;* they are thicker and mostly shorter in the others. In *C. acutus* and the allied species the flagellum of the inner antennæ is longer, while its branches are equally long. In all the other species the flagellum is shorter, and the external branch somewhat longer, than the inner. The antennal lamina is more elongated and enlarged before the middle in the group of *C. acutus;* shorter and enlarged near to the tip in the group of *C. Bartoni;* longer and enlarged in the middle in the group of *C. affinis*. But here are to be found more numerous exceptions, — *C. pellucidus, C. Wiegmanni, C. Carolinus, C. lancifer*, etc., lack the form characteristic of their group.

CAMBARUS. — *Corpore elongato; pedibus quintis branchiis nullis; antennis internis flagello longiori; auro annulari, apice aperto; pedibus maris tertiis, vel tertiis et quartis articulo tertio unguiculatis; pedibus abdominalibus maris bifidis; femina annulo ventrali conico, perforato, separato.*

I. GROUP. (TYPE, C. ACUTUS.)

The third and the fourth pair of legs of the males hooked; rostrum triangular, elongated, with an ante-apical tooth each side, at least in the young; first pair of abdominal legs with the exterior part truncated at the tip with several somewhat dilated incurved corneous teeth, occasionally covered with a pencil of hairs; the interior part terminated in a short, acute, and for the most part outwardly directed spine.

This group seems very natural, if we except some abnormal species, viz. *C. penicillatus, C. Wiegmanni*, and especially *C. pellucidus*.

The body and the hands are more slender and elongated. The flagellum of the inner antennæ has the branches of equal length. The length of the antennæ equals that of the body, or exceeds it; their lamina is elongated, and dilated near the base; the basal joint of the inner antennæ has an inferior spine before the middle. The foreborder of the cephalothorax is angulated behind the antennæ.

In *C. troglodytus* burrowing habits are observed.

It is worthy of remark that in the considerable number of females seen by me, eggs are in no instance attached to the abdomen. Perhaps the females live more retired now than formerly, and are not easily secured. I have seen many females of various species of the other groups with eggs attached to the abdomen.

The species contained in this group are divided into four natural sections, having the following characters:—

1. The rostrum is broad, very long, triangular, with a small spine near the extremity, somewhat, but very slightly, developed (always strongly developed in the young); the postabdomen is as long as the thorax; the hands are elongated; the antennal lamina is long, and enlarged near the base,— *C. acutus* and allied species.

2. The rostrum is broad, very long, triangular, with a strong and acute apical tooth on each side; the postabdomen is longer than the thorax; the hands are elongated; the antennal lamina is long, and enlarged near the base,— *C. spiculifer* and allied species.

3. The rostrum is broad, triangular, not so much elongated, without ante-apical teeth (always developed in the young); the postabdomen as long as the body; the hands are shorter, broader; the antennal lamina is shorter, and enlarged near the tip,— *C. penicillatus* and allied species.

4. The rostrum is broad at the base, very long, with a strong and acute tooth each side; the postabdomen is longer than the thorax; the hands are elongated; the antennal lamina is long, and much enlarged near the tip,— *C. pellucidus*.

The most aberrant species is *C. pellucidus*. Like the other animals living in caves, it is blind. The eyes are atrophied, smaller at the base, conical, instead of cylindrical and elongated, as in the other species. The cornea exists, but is small, circular, and not faceted; the optic fibres and the dark-colored pigments surrounding them in all other species are not developed. The shape of the rostrum is somewhat analogous to that of *C. affinis*, the margins are more parallel at the base. The lamina of the antennæ is long, but strongly dilated nearer to the tip; the epistoma is shorter and broader than in the other species; the basal joint of the inner antennæ has a spine at the tip, which in the other species is always nearer to the base; the foreborder of the cephalothorax is not angulated behind the antennæ as in all other species.

Nevertheless, the number of the hooked legs, the form of the abdominal legs, and the elongated body and hands, exclude *C. pellucidus* from the other groups. Some, no doubt, will prefer to regard *C. pellucidus* as a distinct group or genus, still, as I am convinced, without foundation. The most striking differences consist in the aberrations in the shape of the fore parts and of the limbs of the head. But it seems to be a somewhat well-recognized law in nature (Rathke, Metamorph. Retrograd., p. 125) that if any part is atrophied, or stopped in development, the nearest parts show an abnormal increase of development. This is apparently the case in *C. pellucidus;* the eyes are atrophied, and the rostrum, the fore border of the cephalothorax, the antennal lamina, the basal joint of the inner antennæ, and the epistoma are altered or largely developed.

Similar alterations are not rarely noticed in the insects. The blind soldiers of Termes have the head and the mandibles more developed, the maxillæ and the labium atrophied. Analogous facts are observed in the ants and in the two very nearly related Coleopterous species, *Hylecœtus dermestoides* and *flabellicornis*. In *H. dermestoides* the antennæ are simple, the maxillary palpi extraordinarily developed; in *H. flabellicornis* the antennæ are much developed and the maxillary palpi simple. It would not be difficult to give a greater number of similar examples.

The two species of the third section are not as abnormal as *C. pellucidus*, and they differ only in the two characters before mentioned.

Synopsis of the Species.

1st Section. (See p. 33.)

a. Epistoma rounded in front: *C. acutus, C. Blandingii.*
b. Epistoma truncated in front: *C. Clarkii, C. troglodytes.*

2d Section. (See p. 33.)

a. Areola narrow: *C. fallax, C. LeContei.*
b. Areola broad: *C. spiculifer, C. angustatus, C. versutus.*
(*Incertæ sedis.*): *C. maniculatus.*

3d Section. (See p. 33.)

C. penicillatus: C. Wiegmanni.

4th Section. (See p. 33.)

C. pellucidus.

1. Cambarus acutus *Girard.*

Cambarus acutus Girard, Proc. Acad. Philad., T. 6, p. 91.

Figures on Pl. I., II., and III.
First abdominal legs of the male:
first form, fig. 1 in front; fig. 2 outside; fig. 108 outside viewed more laterally; fig. 106 inside.
second form, fig. 4 in front; fig. 3 tip augmented; fig. 5 outside.
fig. 110 outside, young, 1.7 inch long; fig. 111 outside, 2.7 inches long.
fig. 112 outside, 2.7 inches long, not articulated; fig. 113 outside, 1.4 inch long, not articulated.
var. A, first form, fig. 107 inside; fig. 109 outside.
Venter between the fourth pair of legs of the female, fig. 114, *C. acutus;* fig. 115, var. A.
Rostrum, fig. 116, *C. acutus;* fig. 117, var. A.
Epistoma, fig. 118, *C. acutus;* fig. 119, var. A.
Thoracic line, fig. 124, *C. acutus;* fig. 125, var. A.
Inner sexual parts of the male:
first form, fig. 120; testicles viewed from above, fig. 121.
second form, fig. 122.
Inner sexual parts of the female, fig. 123.
Annulus ventralis of the female, fig. 126 outside; fig. 127 inside.
Antennal lamina, fig. 143, *a*; epistoma, *b*; spine of the second joint of the exterior antennæ, *c*; fig. 144, the same parts for var. B, from New Jersey.

Mas. Rostro triangulari, lato, dimidio longiori, subdeflexo, ante apicem brevem acutum utrinque subsinuato, margine punctato-lineato; supra lævi, subexcavato, basi late foveolato; cretis basalibus extus sulcatis, apice subacutis, fere parallelis, postice callosis convergentibus. Antennis externis corpore æqualibus vel longioribus, articulis duobus basalibus dente externo brevi, subacuto; antennis internis articulo basali ante medium dente infero, acuto; lamina externa rostro longiori, antennarum pedunculo æquali, lata, apice rotundata; margine externo inflato, apice brevi-spinoso. Epistomate brevi lato, excavato, antice rotundato. Pedibus maxillaribus externis intus et subtus barbatis. Thorace postice latiori, densius tuberculato; cephalothorace supra fere lævi, parce-punctato, postice obsolete bicalloso; linea profunda, sinuata, lateribus divisa, spina infera ad antennarum basin apicali, modica; areola angusta, carinata, postice latiori, plana, interdum transverso-impressa; margine postico subexciso. Postabdomine lato, apicem versus subangustiori, lævi, parce-punctato, segmentis utrinque macula obsoleta rubra; segmentis penultimis angulo externo postico recto; lamina media parte apicali breviori, apice rotundata, margine medio exciso; parte basali apice utrinque bispina. Pedibus anticis valde elongatis, corpore interdum longioribus; chela longa, angusta, modice tumida, squamoso-tuberculata; margine interno longo, subrecto, fortiter dentato; digitis longioribus, interno sublongiori, supra planis, subtus medio elevatis; externo recto, interno sinuato; digitis basi tuberculatis, externo tuberculo medio et basali interno; interno basi intus exciso, margine externo basi tuberculato. Carpo longo, latere interno tuberculato, margine interno spinis duabus, antica majori; subtus spinis majoribus duabus anticis, aliisque minoribus internis. Brachio elongato, rostro longiori, extus lævi, intus ante apicem et margine supero tuberculato, spinis duabus anteapicalibus oblique positis; subtus biseriatim spinoso. Pedibus tertiis et quartis articulo tertio unguiculato; pedibus quartis et quintis capitulo basali, quartis elongato-ovali, quintis compresso, laminato. Pedibus abdominalibus brevibus, rectis, validis, apice vix-bifidis; parte externa majori, apice barbata, dentibus tribus fusco-corneis, subincurvis; parte interna dente apicali acuto, obliquo, partem externam fere superanti.

Forma II. differt unguiculis pedum minoribus; pedibus abdominalibus basi articulatis, parte externa fere obtusa, dentibus obsoletis; parte interna dente apicali crassiori, conico.

Mares formæ secundæ variant sæpe brachio rostro breviori, interdum chelis brevibus, valde angustis, digitis rectis, lævibus; rostro forma variabili, latiori, marginibus rectis vel subincurvis, acumine angustiori, utrinque magis sinuato.

Femina differt pedibus anticis chelisque brevioribus, extus lævioribus; ventre inter pedes quartos antice tuberculo majori, postice bi-vel bisbituberculato; annulo ovato, fissura longitudinali, labiis alternato-inflatis. Chela interdum basi rubro-maculata.

Variet. A.

A great number of specimens from Illinois (Lawn Ridge, Basson Ridge, Evanston, Athens, and Peoria) and from Indiana (Mus. Salem), comprising both forms of the male and the female, which differ as follows: The rostrum has the margins not so arcuated at the base, the margins are more straight; the epistoma is often more pointed; the transverse line of the thorax is less sinuated, but usually with a lateral spine. The shape of the first pair of abdominal legs is different; seen sidewise the apex more dilated, not hooked behind, the apical teeth are a little larger, and pointed. The female has the ventral segment between the fourth pair of legs not bituberculated, but with a slightly elevated carina; the ventral segment between the fifth pair of legs is more sharply pointed, its articulation-membrane reaching farther to the tip of the base of the abdominal legs. The hands often have large red basal spots.

I have seen very full-grown females, the males not so full grown as those from New Orleans.

Varietas ? B.

I have seen six adult females from Essex, New Jersey; New York; and Beaufort, North Carolina. At first they seem to belong to another species. The lamina of the antennæ is much smaller at the tip; all have a lateral thoracic spine; the rostrum appears narrower in front of the tip; the tip is more sinuated, with sharper lateral teeth; the hands are smaller and smoother; the femur is not tuberculated on the inner side. But a closer examination of many young and old specimens from the South shows so many analogous forms, that it is impossible, at least as yet, to separate them with certainty. But I confess that they seem, in many respects, to belong to a different species (viz. *C. Blandingii*). Long. corp. 3 ad 4 inch.

Mas maximus long. corp. 6.3; antenn. 5.1; ped. ant. 6.2; chelæ, 3.9.

Patria: New Orleans and Milliken's Bend, Louisiana; Mobile; Charleston, South Carolina; St. Louis, Mississippi bottom; James River, Virginia (Mus. Philad.); Mobile River; Kemper Co., Mississippi (Mus. Philad.).

Var. A. Lawn Ridge, Basson Ridge, Evanston, and Peoria, Illinois; Indiana (Mus. Salem).

Var. B. New Jersey; New York; Beaufort, North Carolina.

Vidi specimina plurima, adulta et juniora.

I have not seen the type of *C. acutus* Gir., but I have no doubt that it is the first form of the species described above. The Museum of Philadelphia possesses two young dry second-form males, labelled "C. acutissimus *Gir.*?" from Kemper Co., Mississippi, the locality mentioned by Mr. Girard for the type. There is no doubt that these males are the young of the species above described, and I think also the veritable *C. acutissimus* Gir., l. c. T. 6, p. 91.

Cambarus acutus is the largest North American species. The most important characters are: the rostrum is one and a half times as long as broad, with a distinct large impression, surrounded by a little elevated part at the base; the thorax is strongly tuberculated, posteriorly dilated, without lateral spine; the areola is impressed, very little carinated in the middle; the external lobes of the two penultimate segments of the postabdomen with the external posterior angle finished in a sharp right angle; the lamina in the middle of the apex is large, the basal part longer than the apical, the terminal margin of which is not very deeply excised in the middle. The antennæ are as long as the body, or longer; their lamina much enlarged in the middle; the external maxillary legs always barbate; the epistoma is transversely elliptical, rounded in front; the anterior legs are very long; the brachium is longer than the rostrum; the hand has large and flat tubercles, which in front are a little hairy; the external margin of the hand and finger is straight; the internal margin nearly straight, strongly denticulated; the mobile finger is sinuated, a little longer than the exterior; the brachium is tuberculated above and inside near the carpus. The female has the venter between the fourth legs behind bi- or bisbituberculated, and a larger flat tubercle near the third legs.

The four species, *C. acutus, C. Clarkii, C. troglodytes, and C. Blandingii* are very similar in size and forms. For *C. Blandingii* see the description of this species. Of the three other species, the thorax is more ovoid, more dilated in *C. acutus;* laterally more compressed in *C. Clarkii;* between the two in *C. troglodytes,* nearly as dilated as in the first, but a little more depressed. The areola is the broadest, but very narrow in *C. acutus,* the narrowest and the most shallow in *C. Clarkii;* in both species the areola is posteriorly much more dilated than anteriorly; in *C. troglodytes* the areola is nearly as broad posteriorly as anteriorly. The thorax is strongly tuberculated in *C. acutus* and *C. Clarkii,* granulated in *C. troglodytes.* The rostrum is most sinuated, and often clearly dentated in *C. Clarkii;* less sinuated and dentated in *C. troglodytes.* The rostrum is nearly plain in *C. troglodytes,* most excavated, with the margins more elevated, in *C. Clarkii; C. acutus* is intermediate. The base of the rostrum shows a different structure, but a little obscure. There is in *C. acutus* and *C. Clarkii* a circular depression, terminated in front by a somewhat rounded elevation in *C. acutus;* in *C. Clarkii* by two oblique straight elevations, united in an obtuse angle; in *C. troglodytes* there is in the circular depression a very flat, central, round elevation or tubercle. The postabdomen is the narrowest and laterally most compressed in *C. Clarkii;* the apical part of the lamina is longer in *C. troglodytes* than in the other species. The hands are the shortest and broadest in *C. troglodytes;* the fingers nearly as long as the hands, in the other species much longer, in *C. Clarkii* they are deflected. The movable annulus in the female of *C. troglodytes* is striking; it is very firmly united with the venter between the fourth legs in the two other species.

Cat. No. 1161, New Orleans, La., L. Agassiz. Mas. Form I. Fem. Specimens, 12.*

Cat. No. 1843, New Orleans, La., L. Agassiz. Mas. very large, Form I. Spec. 1.

Cat. No. 1844, New Orleans, La., L. Agassiz. Mas. Form I. and II. Fem. Spec. 12.*

Cat. No. 1845, New Orleans, La., L. Agassiz. Mas. Form II.; first pair of abdominal legs articulated or not articulated. Spec. 12.*

Cat. No. 291, Mobile, Ala., L. Agassiz. Mas. Form I. and II. Fem. Spec. 12.*

Cat. No. 1846, Mobile, Ala., L. Agassiz. Mas. Form I. and II. Fem. var. thorace læviori. Spec. 12.*

Cat. No. 182, Charleston, S. C., L. Agassiz. Fem. Spec. 1.

Cat. No. 274, St. Louis, Mo., Dr. Engelmann. Mas. young. Spec. 1.

Cat. No. 151, St. Louis, Mississippi bottom, Dr. Engelmann. Mas. Form I. Fem. Spec. 6.

Var. A. Cat. No. 214, Lawn Ridge, Ill., Mr. O. Ordway. Mas. Form I. and II. Fem. Spec. 12.*

* The star signifies that the Museum possesses more than 12 specimens.

Cat. No. 1460, Evanston, Ill., Prof. O. Marcy. Mas. Form I. and II. Spec. 2.

Cat. No. 1820, Basson Pudge, Ill., Mr. Bulten. Mas. Form I. Spec. 1.

Var. B. Cat. No. 191, Essex, N. J. Fem. Spec. 3.

Cat. No. 292, New York. Fem. Spec. 1.

Cat. No. 1821, Beaufort, N. C., Mr. T. Shute. Fem. Spec. 2.

Dry Spec. Mobile, Ala., L. Agassiz. Male Form I. Spec. 1.

Peoria, Ill., Mr. O. Ordway. Male var. A., Form I. Spec. 2.

2. Cambarus Clarkii *Girard.*

Cambarus Clarkii Girard, Proc. Acad. Philad., T. 6, p. 91.

Figures on Pl. I., II., III., and IV

First abdominal leg of the male:

first form, fig. 7 in front; fig. 8 outside.

second form, fig. 9 in front; fig. 10 outside.

young, type of *C. Clarkii*, fig. 99 in front; fig. 100 outside.

development of the first abdominal leg in the young male 0.3 inch long, fig. 133.

more augmented, to show the structure of the knob, fig. 134.

Antennal lamina, fig. 137, *a*; epistoma, *b*; spine of the second joint of the exterior antennæ, *c*.

Tab. IV. mas., first form, New Orleans.

Mas. Rostro triangulari, lato, dimidio longiori, ante apicem acutum brevem utrinque sinuato vel subdentato, margine vix punctato lineato; supra lævi, excavato, basi foveola antice leviter triangulari; cretis basalibus extus sulcatis, apice extus acutis, fere parallelis, postice tuberculoso convergentibus. Antennis externis corpore æqualibus, articulis duobus basalibus dente externo brevi subacuto; antennis internis articulo basali dente infero medio acuto; lamina externa rostro longiori, articulo antennarum tertio æquali, lata, apice rotundata, margine externo inflato, apice brevi-spinoso. Epistomate brevi, duplo latiori, antice truncato, bisinuato, lateribus oblique productis, subsinuatis. Pedibus maxillaribus externis intus et subtus barbatis. Thorace utrinque subcompresso, densius tuberculato, cephalothorace supra lævi, parce punctato, postice obsolete bicalloso; linea profunda, modice sulcata, lateribus fissa, spina infera, ad antennarum basin apicali, acuta; areola angustissima, medio lineari, profunda, postice dilatata, triangulari, plana. Postabdomine lato, compresso, apice subangustiori, lævi, vix punctato, utrinque obsolete rubro, segmentis penultimis angulo externo postico obtuso; lamina media parte apicali vix breviori, basi subattenuata, apice subsinuata; parte basali apice sinuata, utrinque bispinosa. Pedibus anticis elongatis, longitudine corporis. Chela longa, crassiori, squamoso-tuberculata, margine interno longo, subincurvo, fortiter dentato; digitis chelæ longitudine, planioribus, apice subdeflexis, subsinuatis, apicibus acutis, incurvis, lævibus, intus apice spongiosis, basi subdentatis, digito externo tuberculo medio et basali intus majoribus; digito mobili sublongiori, basi intus exciso. Carpo longo, lævi, intus tuberculato, spina media majori; subtus spinis duabus majoribus anticis, aliisque minoribus internis. Brachio rostro longiori, extus lævi, intus ante apicem et margine supero tuberculato, spinis duabus anteapicalibus oblique positis; subtus biseriatim spinoso, spinis internis apicalibus validis. Pedibus tertiis et quartis articulo tertio unguiculato; pedibus quartis et quintis capitulo basali, quartis oblongo-ovali, quintis compresso, laminato.

Pedibus abdominalibus brevibus, rectis, cylindricis, basi et ante apicem attenuatis, vix bifidis; parte externa margine postico dente medio obtuso, apice dentibus brevibus duabus compressis, corneis, latis, rotundato-incurvis; parte interna apice spina fusiformi, acuta.

Forma II. differt antennis chelisque brevioribus, unguiculis pedum minoribus; pedibus abdominalibus basi articulatis, minus attenuatis, parte externa apice fere obtuso, bituberculato, dentibus obscurioribus, nec fusco-corneis; parte interna spina conica breviori.

Mares formæ secundæ variant brachio rostro breviori, lateribus cephalothoracis minus tuberculatis; spina laterali ad lineam transversam (semper fere nulla in Forma I.); forma et latitudine rostri et acuminis variabili, vel marginibus rectis, vel subrotundatis; acumine basi distinctius dentato.

Femina differt antennis chelisque brevioribus, minoribus, minus tuberculatis; ventre inter pedes quartos nudo, non tuberculato; annulo ovali, obtuse conico, fissura longitudinali, labiis antice inflatis, sulcatis, fere bituberculatis.

Long. 3 and 4 unc. Mas maximus; long. 4.2; ped. ant. 4.7; antenn. 4.5; chelæ, 2.6.

Patria: New Orleans. Between San Antonio, Texas, and El Paso del Norte. Vidi specimina multa, adulta et juniora.

This species is very similar to *C. acutus*, but it differs surely; the rostrum is more evidently dentated before the acumen, and the obsolete impression at its base is terminated anteriorly by two oblique elevated lines; the epistoma is truncated and sinuated anteriorly and laterally; the thorax is laterally compressed, the areola linear in the middle; the penultimate segments of the postabdomen with the exterior angle are more obtuse; the apical part of the intermediate lamina is as long as the basal, a little attenuated at the base; the chelæ are shorter and broader; the legs of the postabdomen different; the venter of the fourth legs in the female is without tubercles. There is rarely one spine at the sides of the thorax.

C. Clarkii Girard. I have most carefully compared male and female types collected by the U. S. Mexican Boundary Commission, communicated by Professor Stimpson. They belong, without doubt, to this species. The male is a young specimen of the Forma II. (1.8 unc.

long); the female is smaller. The first abdominal leg of the male, figured by me after the type, shows exactly the shape of the male full-grown Forma II., but not as well finished as it is always found in the young specimens. I have not seen a similar young specimen from New Orleans; the smallest is 2.6 unc. long, but agrees very well. The young of *C. troglodytes*, of which I have seen specimens 0.6 unc. long, are very similar; but *C. Clarkii* differs in having the rostrum exactly triangular and a little attenuated at the tip (it is more dilated, with the margins curved, in *C. troglodytes*); the acumen is longer, more acute (in *C. Clarkii* type $\frac{5}{50}$ unc. left side, $\frac{6}{50}$ right side); the basis of the rostrum has two obsolete elevations connected in an obtuse angle; the lamina of the antennæ is more elongated, smaller at the tip.

In the Museum of the Natural History Society of Boston are two females, together with a great number of apparently very young animals, before described by me.

Cat. No. 1162, New Orleans, La., L. Agassiz. Mas. Form I. and II. Fem. Spec. 12.*

Cat. No. 166, New Orleans, La., L. Agassiz. Mas. Form I. Fem. Spec. 5.

Cat. No. 264, New Orleans, La., Mr. Allen. Mas. Fem., young. Spec. 3.

Cat. No. 1822, Mobile, Ala., L. Agassiz. Mas. Form II., young. Spec. 2.

3. Cambarus troglodytes *Le Conte.*

Astacus troglodytes LeC., Proc. Acad. Philad., T. 7, p. 400.

Figures on Pl. I. and III.
First abdominal legs of the male:
first form, fig. 11 in front, fig. 12 outside.
second form, fig. 13 in front, fig. 14 outside.
Antennal lamina, fig. 141, *a*; epistoma, *b*; spine of the second joint of the exterior antenna, *c*.

Mas. Rostro triangulari, lato, tertia parte longiori, subdeflexo, ante apicem acutum, brevem, paulo barbatum, utrinque leviter sinuato; supra fere plano lævi, utrinque subtiliter marginato, tuberculo obsoleto plano in foveola basali orbiculari; cretis basalibus extus sulcatis, apice subacutis, subparallelis. Antennis gracilibus, corpore paulo brevioribus, articulis duobus basalibus dente externo parvo subacuto; antennis internis articulo basali dente infero medio acuto; lamina externa rostro longiori, articulo antennarum tertio vix breviori, lata, apice vix rotundata, margine externo inflato, apice brevi spinoso. Epistomate lato, antice et utrinque subsinuato (forma variabili, semper brevi, lateribus obliquis). Pedibus maxillaribus intus et basi subtus villosis. Thorace postice latiori, postice subdepresso, granuloso, cephalothorace medio fortius punctato, postice obsolete bicalloso, linea modice profunda et sinuata, lateribus fissa, spina infera ad antennarum basi apicali acuta; areola media angusta, subcarinata, postice latiori, transverse impressa. Postabdomine subangustiori, lævi; segmentis penultimis angulo externo obtuso; lamina media parte apicali vix breviori, antice subrotundata; parte basali apice sinuata, utrinque bi-(vel tri)-spinosa. Pedibus anticis elongatis, corpore vix brevioribus; chela longa, crassiori, squamoso-tuberculata, margine interno longo, subrecto, densius tuberculato et fortiter dentato; digitis paulo longioribus, arcuatis, subcostatis, leviter punctato-lineatis, apicibus acutis, incurvis; intus apice squamosis, basi serratis; digito externo tuberculo medio et basali internis majoribus obtusis; digito mobili sublongiori, basi sinuata, tuberculo majori. Carpo longo, lævi, intus subtuberculato, spina media interna majori; subtus spinis duabus anticis majoribus. Brachio rostro longiori, extus lævi, intus ante apicem tuberculis nonnullis minoribus; margine superiori leviter tuberculoso, spinis duabus majoribus oblique positis; subtus biseriatim spinoso, spinis apicalibus validis. Pedibus tertiis et quartis articulo tertio unguiculato; pedibus quartis capitulo basali, latiori; quintis lamina quadrangulari, parva elevata. Pedibus abdominalibus brevibus, rectis, parte interna intus lata, plana, spina media posteriori, apice bifida; ramo antico brevi, fusiformi, acuto; ramo postico longiori, laminato compresso; parte externa cylindrica, valde bi-attenuata, dente apicali brevi, fusco corneo, triangulari.

Forma II. differt chelis brevioribus, unguiculis pedum minoribus; pedibus abdominalibus basi articulatis, parte interna ramo interno fere obtuso; parte externa dente apicali minori nec fusco corneo; spina thoracis laterali interdum distincta.

Femina differt antennis chelisque brevioribus, minoribus; ventre inter pedes tertios tuberculato, inter pedes quartos nudo; annulo obovali, fissura longitudinali, dentibus alternis, modice inflatis; annulo mobili, nec ventre præcedenti connato.

Long. 3. Mas maximus; long. 3.8; ped. ant. 3.7; antenn. 3.5.

Patria: Charleston, South Carolina; Lawn Ridge, Illinois; Rocky River, Olmsted, Ohio; Georgia.

(Habitat in Georgiæ oryzaceis, ubi spiracula 4 unc. alta format. LeConte.)

I have seen many very young specimens 0.6 inch long.

From Georgia I have seen but four specimens, two males (Forma I.), and two females. The first abdominal legs in the male are a little different in shape. The tip is more recurved, not straight as in the others. Apparently this is the veritable *A. troglodytes* LeC., and the intermediate lamina is always trispinose.

A. troglodytes male type LeConte (Mus. Philad.), with the dimensions given by Mr. LeConte, is identical with the males from Charleston. The abdominal legs are (Forma I.) similar; the lamina is trispinose.

The specimens before mentioned, from Georgia, are not essentially different, though the thorax is more compressed. The female has the areola larger. Some females from Charleston have the lamina also trispinose. It seems not prudent to separate the two species, for the materials are insufficient.

A single male, the largest seen by me, was in the same bottle with *A. obesus*, from Lawn Ridge, Illinois.

The posterior hooks of the abdominal legs of the male exist in the young males, Forma II.; in the very young they are sometimes absent; sometimes they disappear. The fingers are not arcuated in the younger male and female specimens.

A large female (dry), in the Cambridge Museum, communicated by L. R. Gibbes, as *A. Blandingii* Harl. from South Carolina, is *A. troglodytes*.

A. fossarum LeConte. A dry specimen (Mus. Philad.), a female, agreeing very well with the description, does not differ from *A. troglodytes*. It possesses the same compressed thorax, like the specimens from Georgia.

C. Blandingii (Mus. Philad.), from Charleston, is a male, Forma II., of *C. troglodytes*, and perhaps a type of *C. Blandingii* Girard.

Cat. No. 182, Charleston, S. C., L. Agassiz. Male Form I. and II. Fem. Spec. 12.*

Cat. No. 283, Charleston, S. C., Mr. Crady. Male Form I. and II. Fem. Spec. 12.*

Cat. No. 197, Lawn Ridge, Illinois, Mr. O. Ordway. Male Form I. Spec. 1.

Cat. No. 1823, Georgia. Male Form I. and II. Fem. Spec. 4.

Dry spec. South Carolina, L. R. Gibbes. Male, labelled "*A. Blandingii.*" Spec. 1.

Rocky River, Olmsted, Ohio, L. Agassiz. Male. Spec. 1.

Charleston, S. C., L. Agassiz. Male. Spec. 1.

4. Cambarus Blandingii *Harlan.*

Astacus Blandingii Harl, Trans. Amer. Philos. Soc., T. 3, p. 464. Harlan. Med. and Physic. Research, p. 229, fig. 1.

Figures on Pl. I. and III.
First abdominal legs of the male:
first form, fig. 63 in front, fig. 64 outside.
Antennal lamina fig. 140, *a*; epistoma, *b*; spine of the second joint of the exterior antenna, *c*.

Mas. Rostro triangulari, lato, lævi, excavato, marginibus summa basi parallelis, lineato-punctatis; acumine brevi, angusto, acuto, utrinque subsinuato; cretis basalibus validis, extus sulcatis, apice subacutis parallelis, postice calloso-convergentibus. Antennis validis, corpore brevioribus (?secundum Harlani figura), articulis duobus basalibus dente acuto externo; antennis internis articulo basali dente medio infero; lamina rostro paulo longiori, pedunculo antennarum æquali, ante medium latiori, apice angusta, margine externo inflato, apice brevi-spinoso. Epistomate longitudine vix latiori, antice rotundato, lateribus obliquis, angulis lateralibus rectis. Pedibus maxillaribus intus et subtus barbatis. Thorace leviter ovali, grosso-punctato, lateribus granulosis; cephalothorace medio læviori, rarius punctato, postice bicalloso; linea ordinaria profunda, sinuata, utrinque fissa, spina laterali mediocri, spinaque infera apicali; areola angusta, profunda, postice paulo latiori, punctata. Postabdomine thorace vix angustiori, lævi, segmentis penultimis angulo externo postico recto; lamina media parte apicali vix breviori, margine apicali medio vix exciso; parte basali apice utrinque bispinosa. Pedibus anticis valde elongatis, subcylindricis; chela longa depresso-cylindrica, dense squamoso-tuberculata, margine interno longo recto, subdentato; digitis margine interno chelæ æqualibus, intus curvatis, gracilibus, carinatis, punctato-ciliatis, intus squamosis; digito interno paulo longiori; carpo longo, angusto, antice oblique truncato, intus tuberculato, spina interna media, aliaque antica minori, spinis duabus inferis anticis; brachio rostro longiori, extus lævi, intus ante apicem et margine supero tuberculato, spinis duabus anteapicalibus oblique positis. Subtus biseriatim spinoso, spina utrinque antica ad articulationem. Pedibus tertiis et quartis articulo tertio valde unguiculato; pedibus quartis capitulo basali ovali, compresso; quintis perbrevi, acuto. Pedibus abdominalibus validis, rectis; parte interna breviore, recta (dente apicali fracto); parte externa latiori, subcontorta, apice non angustiori; dentibus tribus fusco-corneis, medio longiori, antico lato, contorto, postico parvo, angusto, fere recto.

Long. corp. 3.8 inch; ped. ant. 3.9.

Patria: Camden, South Carolina (mas. Form I.)

I have only seen the type described and figured by Mr. Harlan, preserved dry in the Museum of the Philadelphia Academy, and labelled, "*A. Blandingii* Harlan, Camden, S. C., Dr. Blanding." Camden is situated in the mountains, but Mr. Harlan (in the Trans. Amer. Philos. Soc. l. c.) says: "All the crawfish which I have seen from the Southern States, and I have received specimens from New Orleans and South Carolina, are the same species with that now described." I have most carefully examined several hundred specimens from New Orleans and South Carolina, (the collection in the Museum of Cambridge being very rich for these localities,) but I have not found a single specimen of *C. Blandingii.* The description and the figure given by Mr. Harlan agree very well with his type; but the hand is no broader at the base than seen in the right hand of the figure. The hand is two inches long; the inner finger seems when open 0.1 inch longer than the external, it is as long as the hand, 1 inch.

Cambarus Clarkii and *C. troglodytes* are very similar, but instantly separated since the epistoma is truncated at the tip. *C. Clarkii* differs in having the thorax strongly tuberculated, the areola linear or none; the base of the rostrum with two linear elevations joined in obtuse angle; the second article of the exterior antennæ, with the teeth shorter than its tubercle (as long as in *C. Blandingii* and very acute); the lamina is more enlarged at the tip; the hands broader, shorter, the fingers more arcuated and deflected, more tuberculated (one tubercule on the inside of the external finger in the middle in *C. Blandingii*); the abdominal legs differ also. *C. troglodytes* differs by the same characters.

C. acutus Gir. is very near in the shape and sculpture of the rostrum and epistoma, but the lamina is much larger at the tip; the teeth of the second article are shorter than the tubercle, the hands broader and shorter, the abdominal legs different. I have seen some hundred males of all sizes, but never a male with the abdominal legs analogous to *C. Blandingii.* The body is more tuberculated.

The females from Essex, New Jersey, quoted under *C. acutus* (but it is always difficult to identify females with males) are more similar, the body is not very strongly tuberculated, the lateral spine is evident, the lamina smaller at the tip.

C. Le Contei is very near, but the abdominal legs are different; the shape of the hand is most similar, but the fingers are shorter and straight; the rostrum strongly dentated at the tip, the areola broad. The typical specimen of *C. Blandingii* is very well developed and it does not seem to me to be an abnormal specimen of *C. acutus* with abnormal hands, abdominal legs, and lamina. I cannot help regarding it a good species, perhaps (?) identical with the New Jersey females described provisionally as *C. acutus.*

It is not impossible that *C. Blandingii* LeConte, l. c. p. 400 (Georgiæ et Carolinæ regionibus intermediis), is this species, but in this the linea ordinaria is sulcated as in *C. troglodytes*, and not sulcated in *Le Conte's* species. Erichson gives but a copy from Mr. Harlan's description.

C. Blandingii Gir., l. c. p. 91, without description, is probably *C. troglodytes,* which the Museum possesses from the same locality, Summerville, South Carolina, given by Mr. Girard. (Vide *C. Lecontei.*)

5. Cambarus Fallax *Hagen.*

Figures on Pl. I.
First abdominal leg of the male:
first form, fig. 103 in front, fig. 104 outside.
second form, fig. 105 inside.

Mas. Rostro elongato triangulari, lævi, excavato; acumine subacuto, ciliato, spina utrinque acuta; cretis basalibus validis, parallelis, extus vix sulcatis, apice acutis. Antennis gracilibus, corpore brevioribus, articulis duobus basalibus dente acuto externo; antennis internis articulo basali dente medio infero; lamina rostro pedunculoque antennarum longiori, ante medium latiori, margine externo latius inflato, spina apicali acuta longiori. Epistomate lato, rotundato, antice medio subacuto; pedibus maxillaribus externis intus barbatis. Thorace angusto, compresso, punctato, lateribus scabris; linea profunda, sinuata, lateribus fissa; spina brevi valida, postice leviter barbata, aliaque infera acuta ad antennarum basin; areola plana, punctata, angusta, postice latiori. Postabdomine lato, compresso, thorace longiori, parcepunctato, segmentis penultimis angulo externo subrecto; lamina media parte basali quadrangulari, apice utrinque trispinosa; parte apicali æquali, apice angulis rotundatis. Pedibus anticis longis, gracilibus, angustis; chela elongata, angusta, depresso-cylindrica, leviter squamoso-tuberculata; margine interno longo, recto, subdentato; digitis paulo brevioribus, rectis, subcostatis, intus squamosis; digito mobili margine externo subdentato. Carpo longo, angusto, parce tuberculato, spina antica et media interna breviori; subtus spina antica externa; brachio longiori, sublævi, spinis duabus anteapicalibus oblique positis; subtus biseriatim spinoso, utrinque ad articulationem spina antica acuta. Pedibus secundis chela parce villosa; pedibus tertiis et quartis articulo tertio unguiculato; pedibus quartis et quintis capitulo basali, quartis oblongo majori, quintis compresso, triangulari, erecto. Pedibus abdominalibus validis, brevibus, rectis; parte externa spina anteapicali acuta, obliqua; parte externa dentibus perparvis fusco corneis adpressis.

Forma II., differt pedibus tertiis et quartis unguiculo minori; chela læviori; pedibus abdominalibus basi articulatis, parte interna spina anteapicali fortiori; parte externa apice rotundato; intus ad apicem fortiter sulcatis.

Femina junior differt chela brevi, minori; ventre inter pedes quartos lævi; annulo transversali, valido, fissura longitudinali antica recta, postica dentato-tuberculata.

Long. corp. 2.9; antenn. 2.4; ped. antic. 1.9.

Patria: Florida. Museum Boston Natural History Society.

I have seen only one male of each form (the male of the second form is even a little larger), and two very young females. This species is very near *C. Le Contei*, but differs in the longer thorax, the hands, and the abdominal legs. The legs, especially in the second form, are strongly sulcated on the inner side.

6. Cambarus LeContei *Hagen.*

Figures on Pl. I. and III.
First abdominal leg of the male:
first form, fig. 15 in front; fig. 16 outside.
second form, fig. 17 in front; fig. 18 outside.
Antennal lamina, fig. 145, *a*; epistoma, *b*; spine of the second joint of the exterior antenna, *c*.

Mas. Rostro triangulari, lato, lævi, excavato, marginibus basi fere parallelis, lineato-ciliatis; acumine acuto, ciliato, utrinque spina acuta; cretis basalibus validis, parallelis, extus sulcatis, apice acutis. Antennis corporis fere longitudine, articulis duobus basalibus dente acuto externo; antennis internis articulo basali dente media infera; lamina rostro pedunculoque antennarum sublongiori, ante medium latiori, margine externo latius inflato, spina apicali breviori. Epistomate lato, antice rotundato, angulis externis fere rectis; pedibus maxillaribus externis intus barbatis. Thorace subcompresso, punctato-pubescente, lateribus scabris; linea profunda, vix sinuata, lateribus fissa, spina brevi valida, aliaque apicali infera acuta ad antennarum basin; areola angusta, plana, punctata, postice subito latiori, ante marginem thoracis posticum excisum transverso-impressa. Postabdomine lato, thorace longiori, parcepunctato, segmentis penultimis angulo externo rotundato; lamina media parte basali quadrangulari, apice utrinque tri-(vel quadri-) spinosa; parte apicali breviori, apice leviter emarginato. Pedibus anticis longis, gracilibus, angustis; chela longa, angusta, depresso-cylindrica, ubique squamoso-tuberculata, ciliata; margine interno longo, recto, subdentato; digitis paulo brevioribus, rectis, subcostatis, dense ciliatis, intus squamosis; digito externo dente medio interno minori. Carpo longo, angusto, leviter squamoso-tuberculato, spina antica interna et media majoribus; intus spinoso, spinis duabus anticis validis; brachio longiore, extus sublævi, margine supero et intus ad apicem tuberculato, spinis duabus oblique positis anteapicalibus; subtus spinis nonnullis biseriatis; utrinque ad articulationem spina antica acuta. Pedibus secundis chela intus villosa; pedibus tertiis et quartis articulo tertio unguiculato; pedibus quartis et quintis capitulo basali, quartis oblongo, majori, quintis triangulari, compresso, erecto. Pedibus abdominalibus validis, brevibus, rectis, parte interna apice dente fusco corneo incurvo, spinaque anteapicali longiori transversali; parte externa, æquali, subcontorta medio crassiori, apice dentibus tribus incurvis acutis.

Forma II. differt pedibus tertiis et quartis unguiculo minori, chela angustiori, breviori fere lævi; pedibus abdominalibus basi articulatis, dentibus apicalibus non fusco corneis, condunatis, latioribus.

Femina differt chela breviori, obsolete tuberculosa; ventre inter pedes quartos apice bituberculato; annulo transversali, valido, fissura longitudinali, labiis alternatim crassioribus.

Long. corp. 3.8; antenn. 3.5; ped. antic. 3.2.

Patria: Mobile, Alabama; Pensacola, Florida; Beaufort, North Carolina; Milledgeville, Georgia; Root Pond, Mississippi; vidi 30 specimina.

I had previously considered this species as *C. angustatus* LeConte; but the type in the Philadelphia Museum is surely different (viz. *C. spiculifer*). This species is separated from the similar ones by the short mesothorax, the longer abdomen, and the long, small, and nearly cylindrical hands.

I consider *A. Blandingii* LeConte, l. c. T. 7, p. 400, as probably identical with *C. Lecontei.* The words "linea ordinaria non sulcata" do not agree very well; the transverse line is as sulcated as in *C. troglodytes.* The lamina of the postabdomen is bispinose in Mr. LeConte's species, trispinose in *C. Lecontei.* Still it seems probable that the two species are as likely to be identical with each other as with *C. Blandingii* Harlan.

Cat. No. 201 and 217, Mobile, Ala., L. Agassiz. Male Form I. and II. Fem. Spec. 12.*

Cat. No. 1824, Beaufort, N. C., Mr. T. Shute. Fem. Spec. 1.

Cat. No. 246, Milledgeville, Ga. Fem., and young. Spec. 4.

Cat. No. 307, Root Pond, Miss., Mr. Wailes. Male Form II. Spec. 1.

Cat. No. 249, Pensacola, Fla. Male, Fem., young. Spec. 3.

7. Cambarus spiculifer *Le Conte.*

Astacus spiculifer LeConte, Proc. Acad Philad., T. 7, p. 401.

Figures on Pl. I. and III.

First abdominal legs of the male:

first form, fig. 59 in front; fig. 60 outside.

second form, fig. 61 in front; fig. 52 outside.

Antennal lamina, fig. 147, *a*; epistoma, *b*; spine of the second joint of the exterior antenna, *c*.

Mas. Rostro longo, lævi, excavato, basi obsolete impresso, marginibus punctato-ciliatis, basi parallelis, deinde subconvergentibus; acumine longo, angusto, triangulari, acuto, utrinque spina breviori acuta; cretis validis, modice elevatis, parallelis, extus obsolete sulcatis, apice breviter acutis, postice obsolete inflatis, convergentibus. Antennis validis, corpore paululum brevioribus, articulis duobus basalibus dente externo acuto; antennis internis articulo basali dente medio infero acuto; lamina rostro fere longiori, medio latiori, apice angusta, margine externo latius inflato, spina modica acuta apicali. Epistomate lato, antice triangulari, angulis lateralibus rotundatis; pedibus maxillaribus externis intus barbatis. Thorace leviter ovato, punctato, lateribus leviter granulatis, vel partim tuberculosis; cephalothorace postice obsolete bicalloso; linea profunda, lateribus fissa, utrinque spinis duabus validis acutis; spina antica infera breviori ad antennarum basin; areola lata, ad marginem anticum utrinque impressa, postice latiori, calloso-inflata; margine thoracis postico sinuato. Postabdomine thorace longiori, lato, subcompresso, parce-punctato, segmentis antepenultimis angulis lateralibus fere rectis; lamina media parte basali apice utrinque bispinosa (interdum trispinosa), parte apicali breviori, angulis rotundatis. Pedibus anticis longis, validis; chela longa, lata, subdepressa, ubique tuberculis majoribus obtusis, subtus rarioribus, margine interno subrecto, fortiter dentato; digitis vix brevioribus, planis, subcostatis, punctato-ciliatis; digito interno recto, sublongiore, utrinque dentato; externo incurvo, intus dentato, dente anteapicali majori. Carpo longo tuberculato, extus nudo, spina media interna valida; subtus spinis duabus apicalibus validis, intus bi-vel triseriatim spinoso; brachio longo, margine supero tuberculato, spinis duabus anteapicalibus acutis, subtus spinis biseriatis, anticis utrinque ad articulationem validis. Pedibus tertiis et quartis articulo tertio unguiculato; pedibus quartis et quintis capitulo basali, quartis ovato majori, quintis minori, laminato, erecto. Pedibus abdominalibus validis, apice paululum divisis, parte externa ante apicem angustiori, apice extus barbata, dentibus duobus fuscocorneis incurvis, supero longiori; parte interna fusiformi, apice spina longiori, gracili, subrecta, partem externam non superante.

Forma II. differt chelis minoribus, minus tuberculatis; unguiculis articuli tertii minoribus; pedibus abdominalibus basi articulatis, parte interna fortiori, spina apicali mobili, extus curvata; parte externa apice dentibus conicis, nec fuscocorneis, subincurvis; capitulo basali pedum posticorum minus expresso.

Femina differt antennis brevioribus, chela minori; ventre inter pedes quartos lævi, postice utrinque tuberculo compresso; annulo transverso, sulco antico longitudinali, lumine transverso, profundo, postico.

(Maxim.) Long. corp. 3.6; antenn. 3.3; ped. antic. 3.2.

Habitat: Athens, Georgia; Roswell, Georgia. Vidi multa specimina.

The females from Roswell differ a little in having the venter between the fourth legs not so much tuberculated, and the annulus less open. The males (Forma II.) seem to be identical.

I have seen the male type, Forma II., in the Mus. Philadelphia.

Cat. No. 172, Athens, Ga., Dr. J. LeConte. Male Form I., Fem. Spec. 12.*

Cat. No. 222, Roswell, Ga., Mr. N. A. Pratt. Male Form I., Fem. Spec. 5.

8. Cambarus angustatus *Le Conte.*

Astacus angustatus LeConte, Proc. Acad. Philad., T. 7, p. 401.

Figures on Pl. I. and III.
First abdominal legs of the male.
First form, fig. 65 in front, fig. 66 outside, fig. 67 inside.
Antennal lamina, fig. 146, *a*; epistoma, *b*; spine of the second joint of the exterior antennæ, *c*.

A little dry typical specimen, communicated to the Museum of the Philadelphia Academy by Mr. LeConte, is very difficult to identify with any specimen before me. It is a male (Forma I.), 1.95 inch long, hands 1.2 long, and agrees with the description. It seems to be a young male of *C. spiculifer* or a new species. The differences quoted in the descriptions of *C. spiculifer* and *C. angustatus* are not decisive. The rostrum in *C. angustatus* is described: "valde acuminatum, utrinque versus apicem fortiter et acute unidentatum"; in *C. spiculifer:* "longissime acuminatum, denticulo parvo utrinque ad acuminis basin." The two types show no difference, except that in *C. angustatus* the rostrum is not so narrow before the acumen. I have seen similar differences in *C. spiculifer*. *C. angustatus* is "linea ordinaria apice spina armata," but the same spine exists in *C. spiculifer*. The thorax has but one lateral spine (not at all noticed in the description), and two in *C. spiculifer*. But I have seen *C. spiculifer* with two, with three, and even with one spine. The lamina intermedia of the postabdomen has sometimes three apical spines in *C. spiculifer* as well as in *C. angustatus.* I should not hesitate to unite the two species (*C. spiculifer* as Forma II., and *C. angustatus* as Forma I. of the male), did I not find two differences not so easy to explain.

1. The hands are longer and narrower, not so tuberculated in *C. angustatus;* the fingers a little shorter than the hands, and inside always spongiose. I have seen hands nearly of the same shape in young *C. spiculifer*, but the fingers were always as long as the hands or longer, and not always spongiose, although sometimes a little so at the tip.

2. The first pair of abdominal legs are a little more obtuse at the tip, with the posterior border a little more dilated, and are sulcated on the inside. I confess that these differences are perhaps rather too minute, but the two together seem more important. I should expressly remark, that the type of *C. angustatus* seems well developed, and the hooks in the third and fourth legs strong. Finally, as Mr. John LeConte has seen and observed the species alive, and I have only two single specimens, I prefer to separate *C. angustatus;* a further examination may perhaps bring out more strongly the differences of the two nearly allied species.

"*C. angustatus* is found in Georgia inferiore, in aquæ puræ rivulos inter colliculos arenosos, *C. spiculifer* in Georgia superiore."

9. Cambarus versutus *Hagen.*

Figures on Pl. I. and III.
First abominal leg of the male :
first form, fig. 55 in front ; fig. 56 outside.
second form, fig. 57 in front ; fig. 58 outside.
Antennal lamina, fig. 150, *a* ; epistoma, *b* ; spine of the second joint of the exterior antennæ, *c*.

Mas. Rostro longo, lævi, excavato ; marginibus nudis, basi fere parallelis, deinde subconvergentibus ; acumine angusto triangulari, acuto, utrinque spina valida subrejecta ; cretis basalibus validis, fere parallelis, extus sulcatis, apice spina acuta longiori. Antennis corporis fere longitudine, articulis duobus basalibus dente externo acuto longiori ; antennis internis articulo basali dente medio infero longiori, acuto ; lamina rostro pedunculoque antennarum longiori, media latiori, margine externo lato inflato, spina apicali longiori. Epistomate brevi, lato, antice obtuso triangulari, angulis lateralibus rotundatis ; pedibus maxillaribus externis intus barbatis. Thorace fere cylindrico, lævi, utrinque antice subscabro ; linea profunda, lateribus breviter fissa, spinis utrinque duabus validis, acutis ; areola lata plana, antice posticeque latiori ; margine thoracis postico exciso. Postabdomine thorace vix angustiori, paulo longiori, lævi, segmentis antepenultimis angulo externo subrecto ; lamina media parte basali elongato-quadrangulari, apice utrinque tri- (interdum bi-vel quadri)-spinosa ; parte apicali breviori, antice rotundata. Pedibus anticis modicis, gracilibus ; chela angusta, media inflata, densius tuberculato-squamosa ; margine interno subrecto, dentato ; chela subtus læviori, ad marginem internum distincte sulcata ; digitis chelæ longitudine, angustis, subcarinatis, subsinuatis, intus vix leviter serratis. Carpo longo, lævi, intus tuberculato, apice oblique truncato, spina antica et media internis acutis, longioribus ; subtus spinis duabus anticis majoribus ; brachio breviori, lævi, spinis duabus anteapicalibus oblique positis ; subtus spinis validis biseriatis, utrinque ad articulationem spina antica acuta ; pedibus tertiis et quartis articulo tertio unguiculato ; pedibus quartis capitulo basali ovato, quintis minori laminato, erecto. Pedibus abdominalibus brevibus, modicis, partim intus ciliatis ; parte interna cylindrica, spina anteapicali acuta ; parte externa ante apicem angustiori, apice obtusiori, dentibus tribus internis fusco-corneis, incurvis.

Forma II., differt chelis angustioribus, depresso-cylindricis, rostro interdum magis triangulari ; pedibus abdominalibus basi articulatis, apice obtusioribus, parte interna ante apicem angustiori, spina anteapicali transversali ; parte externa apice obtuso, dentibus obsoletis, nec fusco-corneis ; pedibus tertiis unguiculo minori.

Vidi marem majorem (Forma II.) pedibus abdominalibus basi non articulatis.

Femina differt chelis minoribus; ventre inter pedes quartos apice exciso, tuberculis conicis duobus apice approxinatis; annulo transversali angusto, longitudinaliter fisso.

Maximus. Long corp. 2.6 – 3 ; antenn. 2.5 ; ped. antic. 2 – 2.5.

Patria: Spring Hill, Alabama; ten miles west of Mobile. — Vidi specimina multa.

Sometimes in the larger examples the thorax is more punctulated, and more granulated on the sides.

This species is very similar to *C. Lecontei*, but it differs in having a smaller and more parallel rostrum, a shorter mesothorax, twice as broad an areola, two spines on each side, somewhat shorter but broader hands, its inner margin slightly curved, sulcated beneath, the fingers a little curved, and the sexual parts.

C. versutus, *spiculifer*, *Lecontei*, and *angustatus* (if it be not identical with *C. spiculifer*) form a single group. The mesothorax is short; the abdomen a little longer than the thorax; the areola is broader; the lamina is longer than the pedunculus, and the rostrum long and slender; the spines of the antennal joints are well developed. Besides the differences taken from the sexual organs, *C. Lecontei* and *angustatus* have one lateral thoracic spine, while *C. spiculifer* and *versutus* have two lateral thoracic spines. *C. Lecontei* is separated by long and nearly cylindrical hands; *C. spiculifer*, by strongly tuberculated hands.

Cat. No. 190, Spring Hill, Ala., L. Agassiz. Male Form I. and II. Fem. Spec. 12.*

Cat. No. 1825, ten miles east from Mobile, Ala., L. Agassiz. Male Form I. and II. Fem. Spec. 12.*

10. Cambarus maniculatus *Le Conte.*

Astacus maniculatus LeConte, Proc. Acad. Philad., T. 7, p. 401.

I have not seen this species, which is described by Mr. LeConte as follows: —

Rostrum subplanum, vix concavum, obtusum cum acumine, versus apicem utrinque unidenticulatum. Lamina antennalis pedunculum æquans. Cephalothorax supra punctatus, lateribus sparsim granulosis. Areola suturalis angustissima, stria solum. Dorsum sicut in prioribus. Chela parva, angusta, tuberculato-punctata, margine interiore dentata, digiti recti, carinati, punctati. Carpus intus paucidentatus, dentibus tribus superioribus majoribus spiculæformibus. Brachium punctatum, latere superiore vix serrato, duabus tamen spinis brevibus anterioribus, inferiore seriebus duabus spinularum. Lamellæ caudalis intermediæ pars anterior trispinosa.

Long. corp. 2.3 inch; antenn. 1.3; chelæ, 0.5.

Patria: Habitat cum priore (*C. fossarum*) in fossis Georgiæ inferioris.

The number of the hooked legs is not mentioned, and perhaps this species belongs to the group of *C. affinis*. The "areola suturalis angustissima, stria solum," is a very striking character, suggesting more or less agreement with *C. Clarkii*, *C. Wiegmanni*, *C. lancifer*, *C. obesus*, *C. advena*, and *C. Carolinus*. *C. advena* is otherwise described by LeConte; in *C. Carolinus*, *C. obesus*, and *C. Clarkii* the hands are different; in *C. lancifer* and *C. Wiegmanni* the rostrum differs.

11. Cambarus penicillatus *Le Conte.*

Astacus penicillatus LeConte, Proc. Acad. Philad., T. 7, p. 401.

Figures on Pl. I. and III.
First abdominal legs of the male:
first form, fig. 93 in front; fig. 94 outside.
second form, fig. 95 in front; 96 outside.
Antennal lamina, fig. 149, *a*; epistome, *b*; spine of the second joint of the exterior antennæ, *c*.

Mas. Rostro lato, longo, plano, lævi, apice subdeflexo, marginibus ad acuminis brevis acuti apicem elevatis, convergentibus, antice subito incurvis; cretis vix elevatis, subparallelis, lineato-impressis, muticis. Antennis modicis corpore brevioribus; articulis basalibus duobus dente parvo externo; antennis internis articulo basali dente infero submarginali; lamina brevi, lata, apice fere truncata, margine externo inflato, spina apicali acuta. Epistomate brevi, lato, antice obtuse-triangulari; pedibus maxillaribus externis intus et subtus barbatis. Thorace cylindrico, compresso, punctato, lateribus granuloso; linea modice profunda, subsinuata, lateribus divisa, apice mutica; areola punctata, modica, postice valde dilatata. Postabdomine thoracis longitudine ac latitudine, lateraliter compresso; lamina media parte basali apice utrinque bispina, parte apicali elliptica, vix breviori; segmentis anteapicalibus angulis externis posticis obtusis, rotundatis. Pedibus anticis modicis; chela, latiuscula, punctato-granulosa, margine interno recto, serrato, longe barbato; digitis chelæ æqualibus, rectis, costatis, punctato-ciliatis, intus spongiosis, digito mobili basi extus serrato. Carpo parcepunctato, longiore, extus oblique truncato, margine interno serrato, spina media majori; subtus læviori, spina antica media. Brachio lævi, spinis anteapicalibus parvis; subtus biseriatim spinoso. Pedibus tertiis et quartis articulo tertio unguiculato; pedibus quartis capitulo basali conico, quintis spina basali obtusa. Pedibus abdominalibus rectis, brevibus, apice contortis, subtus medio excisis, apice fere coadunatis; parte interna dente apicali acuto erecto; parte externa apice incurva, internam tegente, dentibus duabus apicalibus corneis perparvis, coadunatis.

Forma II. differt chela non barbata; pedibus abdominalibus magis cylindricis, basi articulatis, parte interna dente apicali extrorsum recurvo, parte externa dentibus non fusco corneis, majoribus, distantibus.

Femina differt chelis minoribus; ventre inter pedes quartos lævi, annulo majori, ovali, sulco longitudinali, alternatim fisso.

Long. 1.8; antenn. 1.3; ped. ant. 1.2.

Habitat: Georgia; Charleston, South Carolina.

Animal paulo villosum. Vidi juniores rostro acutiori, ante apicem utrinque dente acuto, pedibus maris abdominalibus dentibus magis expressis.

The description of *C. penicillatus* LeConte differs somewhat. The words, "Thorax lateribus granulatis," "brachio punctato, spinoso, tuberculato," do not answer very well to the single male, Forma I., which I have seen. But I think the species the same. The tuft of hairs along the inner margin of the hand is very striking.

Cat. No. 250, Charleston, S. C., L. Agassiz. Male, female, young. Spec. 8.

Cat. No. 254, Charleston, S. C., Professor Baird. Male Form I. Fem. Spec. 2.

Cat. No. 279, Georgia, Dr. Jones. Male, young. Spec. 1.

12. CAMBARUS WIEGMANNI *Erichson.*

Astacus Wiegmanni Erichson, Wiegm. Arch., T. 12, p. 99, n. 19.

Figures on Pl. III.
Antennal lamina, fig. 151, *a*; epistoma, *b*; spine of the second joint of the exterior antenna, *c*.

FEM. Rostro lato, modice longo, articulum antennarum secundum vix superanti, plano, punctato, antice sensim angustiori, acumine subito ac breviter triangulari, latitudine fere dimidio breviori; marginibus usque ad apicem elevatis; cretis modice elevatis, postice divergentibus, extus obsolete lineato-impressis, antice muticis. Antennis validioribus, corpore brevioribus; articulis basalibus dente parvo externo; antennis internis dente infero medio acuto; lamina brevi, antice latissima, margine externo inflato, spina apicali brevi, acuta. Epistomate brevi, lato, antice triangulari, acutiori; pedibus maxillaribus intus dense, subtus minus barbatis. Thorace elongato ovato, ubique punctato, lateribus mesothoracis granulosis; linea modica profunda, subsinuata, lateribus divisa, apice mutica; areola punctata, angusta, postice subito latiori. Postabdomine thoracis longitudine, basi thorace latiori, subcompresso, lævi, postice angustiori; segmentis anteapicalibus angulis externis obtusis, subrotundatis; lamina media parte basali apice utrinque bispina parte apicali antice rotundata (? margo deest). Pedibus anticis modicis, dense squamoso-tuberculatis; chela latiuscula, modice inflata, ubique squamoso-tuberculata, margine interno recto serrato; digitis validis, rectis, costatis et punctato-lineatis, extus squamoso-tuberculatis, intus dentatis, tuberculis basalibus validioribus. Carpo squamoso-tuberculato, margine interno dentato; subtus spinis duabus anticis. Brachio lævi, supra et antice tuberculato, subtus biseriatim dentato. Ventre inter pedes quartos nudo, annulo majori, obovato, indiviso, antice subexciso, medio transverso-elevato, postice depresso.

Long. 2.6; antenn. ; ped. ant. 1.7.

Hab.: Mexico. Acad. N. Sc. Philadelphia.

I have seen only one female, which was found by Mr. Pease. Professor Erichson has described a little smaller male (two inches long); the description agrees very well. Erichson remarks that the third pair of legs and the fourth possess a hook.

This species is apparently of the same group as *C. penicillatus*. It differs in the strongly tuberculated hands, the much enlarged lamina of the antennæ, and the small areola. This species and *A. pellucidus* have the lamina of the antennæ most dilated near the tip, all other species of this group have the greatest dilatation behind the middle and nearer the base.

Cambarus Aztecus Saussure, Revue et Magas., T. 9, p. 503, and Mém. Soc. Phys. Genève, T. 14, P. II. p. 460, fig. 23, from Tomatlan (ruisseaux dans les Terres-Chandes), seems to be identical with *C. Wiegmanni*, at least with the female described by me.

13. Cambarus pellucidus *Tellkampf.*

Astacus pellucidus Tellkampf, Mueller Archiv. 1844, p. 383. — Erichson, Wiegm. Archiv., T. 12, p. 95, n. 14.

Figures on Pl. I., III., and VI.
First abdominal legs of the male:
first form, fig. 68 in front, fig. 69 outside.
second form, fig. 70 in front, fig. 71 outside.
Antennal lamina, fig. 148, *a*; epistoma, *b*; spine of the second joint of the exterior antenna, *c*.

Mas. Rostro lato, longo, lævi, subexcavato, foveola basali, latiori, marginibus modice elevatis, subconvergentibus, utrinque valde excisis, spina valida, acuta, subrejecta; acumine longo, angusto, acuto; cretis perparvis, fere parallelis, extus impressis, antice spina valida acuta. Antennis corpore longioribus, articulis duobus basalibus dente externo valido; articulo basali internarum dente infero subapicali acuto; lamina rostro fere longitudine, sat lata, ante apicem latiori; margine externo paulo rotundato, inflato, spina apicali acuta. Epistomate brevi, lato, subexcavato basi vix angustiori obtuse triangulari, dente medio antico interdum producto. Pedibus maxillaribus externis intus barbatis.

Thorace fere cylindrico; mesothorace longiori, postice paulo angustiori; parce punctato, lævi, lateribus subgranulosis; cephalothorace utrinque spinis nonnullis acutis; linea profunda, non sinuata, serie postica spinarum acutarum, spinaque acuta antica infera ad antennarum basin; areola sat lata, plana, lævi. Postabdomine latitudine thoracis, compresso, lævi, apice non angustiori, angulis segmentorum externis rectis; lamina media parte apicali longa elliptica, parte basali apice utrinque bispinosa. Pedibus anticis longis gracilibus, chela longa, angusta, depresso-cylindrica, subpunctata, margine interno longo, recto, dentato; margine externo subdentato; digitis vix longioribus, rectis, gracilibus, subcostatis, basi subdentatis. Carpo longo, subcylindrico, intus tuberculato, spina media acuta; subtus spinis duabus anticis acutis, serie interna tuberculosa. Brachio longo, margine supero tuberculoso, spinis duabus anteapicalibus, oblique positis; subtus spinis acutis biseriatis. Pedibus tertiis et quartis articulo tertio unguiculato; pedibus quartis capitulo basali compresso, dilatato. Pedibus abdominalibus modicis, rectis, apice contortis; parte interna fortiori, cylindrica, apice membranacea, triangulari, acuta, subincurva; parte externa vix breviori, apice cornea, subrecurva, triangulari. Oculis occultis, cornea parva, indivisa.

Forma II. Pedibus abdominalibus basi articulatis, similibus, apice obtusis, nec corneis.

Femina differt chelis minoribus; ventre inter pedes quartos nudo, annulo rotundato, clauso, medio carinato.

Long. corp. 2.6 and 3.2; antenn. 3.2 and 3.4; ped. ant. 2.1.

Hab.: Mammoth Cave, Kentucky.

I have seen thirty-eight specimens, old and young.

The Museum possesses a full-grown female of *C. Bartonii*, with the eyes well developed, found in the Mammoth Cave.

I have given the peculiarities of this abnormal species in the introduction to this genus. I remark that in the second-form males the abdominal legs are often not articulated, and that the hooks on the third and the fourth set of legs are less developed. I have seen a few specimens with the hooks on the fourth pair of legs much less developed; in one specimen, even, they are entirely wanting. This observation justifies me, perhaps, in placing *C. pellucidus* as the last species of this group, and as somewhat allied to the following group of *C. affinis*.

Cat. No. 193, Mammoth Cave, Kentucky. Male Form I. and II. Fem. Spec. 12.*

Cat. No. 225, Mammoth Cave, Kentucky, Professor Baird. Male Form I. and II. Fem. Spec. 12.*

Cat. No. 1826, Mammoth Cave, Kentucky. Male. Fem. Spec. 5.

Cat. No. 1827, Mammoth Cave, Kentucky. Male, very large. Spec. 1.

Dry Spec. Mammoth Cave, Kentucky. Male. Fem. Spec. 2.

II. GROUP. (Type, C. affinis.)

The third legs of the males hooked; rostrum subquadrangularly elongated, with an anteapical tooth on each side, at least in the young; first pair of abdominal legs bifid, elongated, straight and acute at the tip.

This group seems very natural, if we except two abnormal species, *C. immunis* and *C. extraneus*. *C. lancifer* is to be considered in some degree as an exaggerated form of this group.

Well-developed hooks always appear on the third pair of legs of the male; on the fourth pair they are never to be found; in very rare instances the second pair shows similar incipient hooks more largely developed (as in *C. virilis*).

The rostrum is exceedingly long, more than three times longer than broad, in *C. lancifer*. In all the other species the rostrum is twice, or less than twice as long as broad, of a more subquadrangular form; excavated, the margins thickened and parallel (*C. affinis*), or concave on the sides (*C. juvenilis* and *C. placidus*), or flattened, more or less straight on the sides, in the other species. The apical tooth and the two lateral teeth are all well developed, at least in the young. In *C. immunis* alone the shape of the rostrum is very different in the full-grown species. The rostrum is conical, short, and toothless, as in the third group (*C. Bartonii*); nevertheless, according to the form of the abdominal legs, it belongs to the group of *C. affinis*.

The foreborder of the cephalothorax is strongly angulated behind the antennæ in *C. lancifer*, *C. extraneus*, *C. immunis*, and *C. affinis*, straight or slightly notched in all the other species. This character serves to separate the species otherwise related to *C. affinis* into two sections of equal value.

The first pair of abdominal legs is always strongly bifid, the tips much elongated and acute. In *C. lancifer*, while the tips are not so much elongated, they are somewhat flattened, but apparently of the shape characteristic of this group. A remarkable exception is to be found in *C. extraneus*, which has the first pair of abdominal legs of the shape peculiar to the third group (*C. Bartonii*); but the rostrum and other characters prevent me from placing them otherwise than in the group of *C. affinis*.

The body and the hands in the species of the second group are shorter and broader, except in *C. lancifer*, which more nearly resembles the species of the first group. The flagellum of the inner antennæ has the internal branch visibly narrower, and sometimes even a little shorter, than the external branch. The lamina of the antennæ is smaller, shorter, and dilated in the middle, except in *C. lancifer*, the lamina of which has exactly the form described in the first group. The epistoma is mostly truncated before in front. The basal joint of the inner antennæ has a spine beneath, in the middle, or nearer the tip.

As yet burrowing habits have not been observed in the species belonging to this group. But perhaps *C. obscurus* is identical with *Astacus fossor* Rafinesque, which burrows in meadows and milldams.

The species contained in this group are divided into four sections, or perhaps they more fitly form one natural group and three abnormal or exaggerated species, which may be described in the following terms: —

1. The rostrum is very long and acute; the lamina of the antennæ elongated, dilated near the base; the hands are narrow and elongated; the first abdominal legs somewhat flattened at the tip. (*C. lancifer.*)

2. The rostrum is more subquadrangular; the lamina of the antennæ small, short, dilated in the middle; the hands are shorter and broader; the first abdominal legs acute at the tip. (*C. affinis* and allied species.)

3. The rostrum is short, conical, toothless; the other characters are as in the foregoing groups. (*C. immunis.*)

4. Characters as in the groups of *C. affinis*, but the first abdominal legs recurved at their extremity, the tip of which is rounded (as in *C. Bartonii*).

Synopsis of the Species.

1st Section.

1. *C. lancifer.*

2d Section.

2. *A.* The margins of the excavated rostrum thickened.
   - *a.* The margins straight, front border of the cephalothorax angulated: *C. affinis.*
   - *b.* The margins concave, front border of the cephalothorax not angulated: *C. juvenilis* and *C. placidus.*

   B. The margins of the flattened rostrum not thickened, front border of the cephalothorax not angulated.
   - *a.* The rostrum carinated at the tip: *C. propinquus.*
   - *b.* The rostrum not carinated: *C. virilis, C. rusticus, C. obscurus.*

3d Section.

3. *C. immunis.*

4th Section.

4. *C. extraneus.*

I have already mentioned that the species more closely related to *C. affinis* are separated into two sections, one with the front border of the cephalothorax angulated, — *C. affinis, C. lancifer, C. immunis, C. extraneus;* the second with the front border straight or slightly notched, — *C. juvenilis, C. placidus, C. propinquus, C. virilis, C. rusticus, C. obscurus.* The latter section is very natural, and perhaps it would be preferable to follow this arrangement in the separation of the species described.

14. Cambarus lancifer *Hagen.*

Figures on Pl. I. and III.
First abdominal legs of the male:
first form, fig. 86 in front; fig. 87 outside.
Antennal lamina, fig. 159, *a*; epistoma, *b*; spine of the second joint of the exterior antenna, *c*.

Mas. Rostro lato, longo, lævi, profunde excavato, longissime acuminato, marginibus parallelis, ad acuminis apicem ciliatis; acumine rostro longiori, angusto, acuto, recto, antennarum pedunculo longiori, basi utrinque spina valida; cretis basalibus rostro coadunatis parallelis, modicis conicis, extus vix sulcatis, apice acutis. Antennis corpore paulo brevioribus, gracilibus, articulis basalibus elongatis, articulo primo dente externo longiori, acuto, articulo secundo dente parvo acuto; antennis internis articulo basali dente medio infero acuto. Lamina longa, rostro æquali, angusta, ante medium latiori, deinde sensim attenuata, margine externo sinuato, inflato, apice acuto. Epistomate brevi, lato, antice obtuso-triangulari, angulis lateralibus rotundatis. Pedibus maxillaribus intus barbatis. Thorace cylindrico, cephalothorace supra longiori, lævi, sub-pubescente; linea profunda, non sulcata, lateribus fissa, spina valida, acuta, intus barbata; spina antica infera ad antennarum basin parva; areola media nulla, antice spatio triangulari parvo, postice majori plana. Postabdomine thoracis latitudine, subtiliter punctato, segmentis antepenultimis angulo externo acutiori; lamina media parte apicali breviori, antice leviter rotundata, media subsinuata; parte basali apice utrinque spina unica valida. Pedibus anticis longis, gracilibus, depresso-cylindricis, subpubescentibus; chela longa, angusta, subdepressa, marginibus parallelis, interno longo, recto; digitis brevioribus, rectis, intus squamosis; carpo longo, leviter oblique truncato, spina interna antica brevi, acuta; subtus spina antica externa valida, acuta; brachio longo, spina anteapicali acuta; subtus spina interna antica, aliaque externa media brevioribus. Pedibus tertiis articulo tertio unguiculato; pedibus quartis tuberculo perparvo basali, quintis capitulo basali annulari. Pedibus abdominalibus brevibus, validis, apice bifidis, contortis; parte interna cylindrica, apice subito subangustiori, extus curva, laminata, obtusa; parte externa fortiori, apice subito subangustiori, fusco cornea, intus curva, laminata, obtusa.

Long. corp. 2.8; antenn. 2; ped. antic. 2.

Patria: Root Pond, Mississippi.

Species valde insignis; vidi marem unicum, Forma I., pedibus abdominalibus basi non articulatis, apice fusco corneis, rostro acumine longissimo.

Cat. No. 306, Root Pond, Miss., Mr. Wailes. Male Form I. Spec. 1.

15. Cambarus affinis *Say*.

Astacus affinis Say, Journ. Philad. Acad., T. 1, p. 168, n. 3. — Harlan., Med. Physic. Researches, p. 230, fig. 2.

Figures on Pl. I., III., and V.
First abdominal legs of the male (full-grown *C. Pealei*):
first form, fig. 84 in front, fig. 85 outside.
Common size:
first form, fig. 19 in front, fig. 20 outside.
second form, fig. 21 in front, fig. 22 outside.
Antennal lamina, fig. 152, *a*; epistoma, *b*; spine of the second joint of the exterior antenna, *c*.
Pl. V. Full-grown female (*C. Pealei*) from Maryland, Havre de Grace.

Mas. Corpore pubescente; rostro lato, parallelo, basi media late excavata, utrinque ad marginem linea impressa, ciliata; acumine angusto, triangulari, acuto, parti dilatatæ fere æquali, marginato, apice subrecurvo, basi utrinque spina acuta longiori; cretis validis, extus sulcatis, parallelis, spina apicali longiori. Antennis validis thoracis longitudine; articulis duobus basalibus dente externo acuto longiori; antennis internis articulo basali dente infero medio acuto longiori; lamina longa, rostri longitudine, lata ad apicem attenuata, margine externo late inflato, spina apicali valida. Epistomate lato eliptico, basi angustiori. Pedibus maxillaribus externis intus, basi subtus villosis. Thorace ovoideo, punctato-pubescente, lateribus leviter, antice magis granulosis; cephalothoracis lateribus spinis nonnulis minoribus; linea profunda, vix sinuata, utrinque fissa, spina acuta, valida; spina apicali, infera, acuta; areola modica, plana, antice posticeque æque latiori. Postabdomine thorace longiori, lato, fere lævi, segmentis penultimis angulis externis subrectis; lamina media parte apicali breviori rotundata; parte basali utrinque apice bispina; lamina laterali usque ad marginem costata; lamina externa toto margine intermedio dentato. Pedibus anticis brevibus, chela brevi, angusta, depressa, punctato-ciliata, margine interno subrecto, serrato, margine externo lineato; digitis paulo longioribus, rectis, subcostatis, margine interno recto, spongioso; chela subtus parce punctata, digitis magis ciliatis. Carpo longo, oblique truncato, punctato-ciliato, spina media aliaque antica minori, internis acutis; subtus spinis duabus acutis validis. Brachio brevi, lævi, spinis duabus anteapicalibus acutis validis, oblique positis; subtus spinis nonnullis validis, acutis, biseriatis. Pedibus tertiis articulo tertio articulato; pedibus quintis capitulo basali annulari. Pedibus abdominalibus, brevibus, validis, rectis, subcontortis, apice breviter bifidis; parte interna cylindrica, apice cornea, laminata; parte externa æquali, apice recurva, cornea, acuta.

Forma II. differt pedibus abdominalibus basi articulatis, apicibus nec fusco corneis, parte interna conica, acutiori, externa obtusiori recurva.

Femina differt ventre inter pedes quartos lævi; annulo obovato, valido, lumine postico transversali, sulco antico longitudinali, fere bituberculato.

Long. corp. 3; antenn. 1.4; ped. antic. 1.9.

Very old specimens: Long. corp. 4.7; antenn. 2.8; ped. ant. 3.5.

Patria: Reading, Schuylkill River, Philadelphia; Pittsburg, Pennsylvania; New Jersey. Many very young specimens from the Niagara and Lake Erie. The very old specimens from New York; Havre de Grace, Maryland; from the Potomac at Washington; Carlisle, Pennsylvania.

The abdominal legs of the first form of the male vary a little in the shape of the interior tip, which is more or less acute. I have figured both; the more acute one is taken from the largest specimens, but it is also found in the younger. The obtuse tip is figured from one of intermediate age.

The young are similar to *A. propinquus* (*vide* that species).

The full-grown and very old specimens, described by Mr. Girard as *Cambarus Pealei*, differ in the following points:—

MAS. Corpore densius punctato-pubescente; rostro latitudine duplo longiori, leviter excavato, basi foveola lata, profundiori; marginibus lateralibus inflatis, spinis anteapicalibus validis, subrejectis; lamina antennarum margine externo subsinuato. Epistomate brevi, lato, antice obtuso-rotundato, angulis lateralibus acutioribus. Thorace lateribus magis granuloso; cephalothoracis spinis acutioribus; linea profunda, utrinque fissa, spina duplici valida acuta aliisque minoribus; spina antica infera rejecta; areola punctato-ciliata. Pedibus anticis validis; chela forte ciliato-punctata, margine interno subincurvo, dentato, supra et subtus sulcato, digitis vix longioribus, planis, intus et digito mobili extus dentatis; carpo spina interna media valida; brachio spinis nonnullis anteapicalibus, nonnullisque minoribus anticis, omnibus acutis; subtus utrinque spina ad articulationem valida. Annulo feminæ utrinque tuberculo ad sulcum longitudinalem valido.

Six very old and full-grown specimens from Havre de Grace, Maryland, agree so very well with the description given by Mr. Thomas Say, that they are doubtless *Astacus affinis* Say. A full-grown male from the Potomac, communicated by the Philadelphia Academy and labelled "*C. Pealei* Girard?" is identical with the specimens from Havre de Grace. Girard's species was from the Potomac, and "the fingers fasciate with green near the tips" are also described by Mr. Thomas Say. I have seen male and female from Reading, Schuylkill River, collected by Professor Baird, labelled as *C. affinis* Girard, and communicated as types from the Smithsonian collection by Professor W. Stimpson. The male belongs to the second form; the specimens are young, with only one lateral thoracic spine; in other respects they do not differ. I have no doubt that they are young of the species described above; Mr. Girard's description of *C. affinis* being made from specimens from Reading, and of *C. Pealei* from those of the Potomac, he was perhaps induced by this difference (though he does not say so) to refer the individuals to two species. The other differences given by him, namely, the longer antennæ, the broader area, the much less developed lateral spine of the rostrum, have no decisive value.

The *Astacus limosus* Rafinesque, Amer. Monthl. Mag., T. 2, p. 42, from the muddy banks of the Delaware, is apparently the same species, as quoted before by Mr. Girard. Rafinesque describes "a thorn of each flank" and gives the extreme dimensions "three to nine inches." I have seen specimens three inches long with only one thorn upon a side, and I have no doubt about their identity. The largest specimen seen by me is about five inches long. Nearly all younger specimens (three inches long) are bearded at their articulations, as quoted by Rafinesque; the larger specimens show much less hair. The description of *A. limosus* was published in November, 1817, of *A. affinis* in December, 1817, one month later. But the description of *A. affinis* is so perfect, that of *A. limosus* so imperfect, that it would be more suitable to retain the name given by Mr. Thomas Say, although the other has the priority.

The identity of *A. affinis* Erichs., Wiegm. Archiv, T. 12, p. 96, n. 15, is probable. His description contains no different indication, but gives no security. *A. Bartonii* Milne Edw., Hist. Crust., T. 2, p. 331, n. 2, is apparently *C. affinis*. The typographical error in the quotation of the figures by Mr. Harlan has misled Mr. Milne Edwards, as Erichson remarks. The types of *A. Bartonii* Gibbes, in the Philadelphia Academy, are *C. affinis*.

Cat. No. 164, Havre de Grace, Md., Mr. T. R. Williams. Male Form I. Fem. Spec. 4.

Cat. No. 180, Havre de Grace, Md., Mr. T. R. Williams. Male Form I. Spec. 2.

Cat. No. 163, New Jersey, Mr. Abry. Male. Fem., young. Spec. 3.

Cat. No. 162, Schuylkill River, Pa., Mr. J. H. R. Male. Fem., young. Spec. 6.

Cat. No. 179, Niagara, N. Y., L. Agassiz. Male. Fem., young. Spec. 12.*

Cat. No. 177, Carlisle, Pa. Male. Fem., young. Spec. 2.

Cat. No. 270, New York, Mr. Pike. Fem. Spec. 1.

16. Cambarus virilis *Hagen.*

Figures on Pl. I., II., III., and VIII.
Antennal lamina, fig. 155, *a*; epistoma, *b*; spine of the second joint of the exterior antenna, *c*.
First abdominal legs of the male:
first form, fig. 23 in front; fig. 24 outside; figs. 25, 26 variety, outside.
second form, fig. 27 in front; fig. 28 outside.
Inner sexual parts of the male:
first form, figs 128, 129 side; fig. 132 viewed more from above.
second form, figs. 130, 131 side.
Pl. VIII. Male, first form: *a* variety A.

Mas. Rostro lato, fere duplo longiori, subexcavato, marginibus parallelis, antice vix convergentibus, punctato-lineatis; ante apicem utrinque subito sinuato, acumine triangulari, acuto, rostri latitudine non longiori, angusto, angulo basali laterali corneo, obtuso vel subacuto; cretis basalibus extus sulcatis, parum elevatis, parallelis, antice truncatis, subacutis. Antennis corpore brevioribus, articulis duobus basalibus dente externo, parvo, subacuto; antennis internis articulo basali dente infero medio acuto interno; lamina rostri longitudine, lata, margine externo inflato, apice brevi spinoso. Epistomate longitudine dimidio latiori, antice truncato, angustiori, acumine medio brevi, lateribus obliquis, subexcavato. (Forma epistomatis variabili, antice lateribusque margine vel recto, vel sinuato, vel exciso; angulis obtusis vel rotundatis.) Pedibus maxillaribus externis intus et subtus villosis. Thorace leviter ovato, subdepresso, parce sed distincte punctato, lateribus scabris, cephalothorace medio fere lævi; linea profunda modice sinuata, utrinque fissa, spina brevi, valida; spina antica infera subnulla; areola plana, punctata, medio angusta, postice magis dilatata. Postabdomine lato, thoracis longitudine, parcepunctato, segmentis penultimis angulo externo obtuso; lamina media parte apicali breviori, angulis rotundatis; parte basali apice sinuata, utrinque spinis duabus validis. Pedibus anticis brevibus, validis; chela lata, planiori, obsolete punctata, intus tuberculis biseriatis dentata; digitis dimidio longioribus, latis, planis, costato-lineatis, fortiter punctatis; interno recto, basi extus et intus tuberculoso-dentato; externo basi margine interno tuberculoso, subtus barbato, margine externo lævi, apice subincurvo; carpo latitudine vix longiori, extus oblique truncato, sublævi, spina interna media majori, aliaque basali minori; subtus spinis duabus anticis validis; brachio brevi, lævi, spinis duabus anteapicalibus oblique positis, obtusis; subtus spinis biseriatis acutis. Pedibus tertiis articulo tertio unguiculato; pedibus quintis capitulo basali brevi. Pedibus abdominalibus longis, subcontortis, longe bifidis, apice acutis, incurvis; parte externa longiori, basi crassiori; parte interna apice compresso-dilatata, acuta vel obtusiori.

Forma II. Pedibus abdominalibus basi articulatis, apicibus paululum divisis, crassioribus, cylindricis, minus incurvis.

Femina differt chelis minoribus; ventre inter pedes quartos lævi, annulo magno, fere cordiformi, fissura transversa, lata, profunda, margine tumido, antice fisso.

Variat interdum angulis rostri ad acuminis basin longioribus brevispinosis; rostri interdum angustiori, acumine longiori; lamina antennarum rostro longiori.

Long. 3.2; long. antenn. 2.4; long. ped. antic. 2.7.

Patria: Lake Superior; Lake Winnipeg; Saskatchavan and Red River, British America, and Toronto, Canada; Quincy, Illinois; Davenport and Burlington, Iowa; Miami River, Dayton, Ohio; Osage River, Missouri; Sugar River, Wisconsin (Mus. Salem); Texas.

I have seen the male of both forms from Lake Superior and from Illinois.

Var. A.

I have seen many full-grown male (Forma II.) and female examples from the Osage River, Missouri, and male and female from the Miami River, Dayton, Ohio, in the Philadelphia Museum, which I cannot yet separate specifically. The rostrum is smaller anteriorly, the thorax seems not so much dilated and less punctated, the areola is a little smaller; the fingers are more separated, the exterior more notched at the base interiorly; the carpus is trispinose beneath at the apex, the third spine is between the great middle interior spine and the two ordinary apical spines; the legs composing the third pair are not so much hooked, and those of the abdomen are similar to those of the second form described.

The male (Forma I.) and female from Davenport, Iowa, are in form and specific character doubtless identical with the examples from Lake Superior; but they agree more nearly with the specimens from the Osage River in the form of the rostrum and the greater development of the spines; the third spine on the carpus is more or less visible.

It is likewise impossible to separate the males and females from Texas. The rostrum is intermediate, but more similar to the Osage examples; the abdominal legs (Forma I.) are of the typical form; the carpus is trispinose, but in some examples from Lake Superior there is a similar third spine very little developed. One male is larger: Long. corp. 4.1; long. ped. antic. 3.7; long. chelæ, 2.2. In this male the fingers are more elongated.

The examples from Burlington, Iowa, are similar to the Texas examples. The male has a little hook at the third joint of the second pair of legs, but a similar monstrosity is not very uncommon. Accidentally the spines on the rostrum are more or less obliterated.

Cat. No. 1151, Lake Superior, L. Agassiz. Male Form I. and II. Fem. Spec. 12.*

Cat. No. 194, Lake Superior, L. Agassiz. Male Form I. and II. Fem. Spec. 12.*

Cat. No. 203, Lake Superior, L. Agassiz. Male Form II. Fem. Spec. 6.

Cat. No. 1828, Lake Winnipeg, British America, Mr. S. H. Scudder. Male. Fem. Spec. 12.*

Cat. No. 1829, Red River, British America, Mr. S. H. Scudder. Male. Fem. Spec. 12.*

Cat. No. 1830, Saskatchavan River, British America, Mr. S. H. Scudder. Male. Fem. Spec. 4.

Cat. No. 196, Quincy, Ill., Dr. Watson. Male. Fem. Spec. 12.*

Var. A.

Cat. No. 1831, Osage River, Dr. Stolley. Male Form II. Fem. Spec. 12.*

Cat. No. 1832, Osage River, Dr. Stolley. Male Form II. Fem. Spec. 12.*

Cat. No. 192, Osage River, Dr. Stolley. Male Form I. Spec. 1.

Cat. No. 171, Burlington, Iowa. Male Form I. Fem. Spec. 3.

Cat. No. 200, Texas, Dr. Stolley. Male Form I. Fem. Spec. 12.*

Cat. No. 207, Texas, Dr. Stolley. Male Form I. Fem. Spec. 4.

Cat. No. 1833, Davenport, Iowa. Male Form I. Fem. Spec. 3.

Dry Spec., Lake George, L. Agassiz. Male. Spec. 1.

17. Cambarus placidus *Hagen.*

Figures on Pl. I. and III.
First abdominal legs of the male:
first form, fig. 76 in front; fig. 77 outside.
not articulated second form, fig. 78 in front; fig. 79 outside.
Antennal lamina, fig. 158, *a*; epistoma, *b*; spine of the second joint of the exterior antenna, *c*.

This species is intermediate between *C. virilis* and *C. juvenilis*. It lives in the same localities, — Texas, Tennessee, and Quincy, Illinois. In its general form, more cylindrical thorax, smaller and more deeply sulcated rostrum, with the margins more thickened, it resembles *C. juvenilis;* the abdominal legs of the male (Forma I. and II.) are very similar to those of *C. virilis*, though in one male the posterior hook is slightly evident; nevertheless, the forehands are very dissimilar, more slender, much longer, not so much punctated, especially on the fingers, which are flattened; the inner margin of the hands is very little tuberculated; the fingers are more separated at the base, while the external one is not barbated; a few females from Tennessee have little hairs, and are scarcely tuberculated at the inner margin, though sometimes they are much elongated; the carpus is bispinose beneath, the spines often being very obtuse, especially the interior ones; the biseriated spines beneath the brachium, except the two apical ones, are nearly or quite obliterated, as in *C. juvenilis*. The external maxillary legs are not barbated beneath.

The largest male: Long. corp. 3.5; long. ped. antic. 2.5.

Patria: Lebanon, Tennessee; Quincy, Illinois; Texas.

I have seen more than twenty examples, male (Forma I. and II.) and female. In the males, Forma II., the abdominal legs are not articulated at the base.

Cat. No. 289, Lebanon, Tenn., Mr. J. M. Safford. Male Form I. and II. Fem. Spec. 12.*

Cat. No. 296, Quincy, Ill., Dr. Watson. Male Form I. Spec. 1.

Cat. No. 170, Texas, G. Stolley. Male Form I. and II. Fem. Spec. 12.*

18. Cambarus juvenilis *Hagen.*

Figures on Pl. I. and III.
First abdominal legs of the male:
first form, fig. 29 in front; fig. 30 (Tab. II.) viewed more outwardly; fig. 31 outside.
second form, fig. 32 in front; fig. 33 outside.
Antennal lamina, fig. 157, *a*; epistoma, *b*; spine of the second joint of the exterior antenna, *c*.

Mas. Rostro angusto, longiori, sulcato, marginibus basi divergentibus, crassioribus, costato-lineatis; acumine triangulari, angusto, acuto, sinuato, spina utrinque brevi fusco-cornea, subrejecta; cretis subparallelis, vix elevatis, sulcatis, spina antica brevi, fusco-cornea. Antennis corpore paulo longioribus, articulo basali dente externo brevi, articulo secundo dente subnullo; articulo antennarum internarum basali dente infero acuto, magis apicali; lamina parva, rostro fere longiori, angusto, margine externo late inflato, apice longius spinoso. Epistomate lato, antice obtuso-angustiori, lateribus sinuatis, angulis basalibus paulo prominentibus. Pedibus maxillaribus externis intus summaque basi subtus villosis. Thorace fere cylindrico, subdepresso, punctato, punctis ad rostri basin profundis crebrioribus, lateribus leviter granulosis; linea modice profunda, vix sinuata, utrinque fissa, spina parva acuta; spina antica infera nulla; areola angusta, plana postice paulo latiori. Postabdomine thoracis latitudine, fere lævi, segmentis penultimis angulo externo obtuso; lamina media parte apicali breviori, rotundata, parte basali apice angustiori, sinuata, utrinque bispina. Pedibus anticis latis, brevibus; chela lata, depressa, ubique grosso-punctata, margine interno brevi, incurvo, tuberculis squamosis serrato; digitis longioribus, rectis, costatis, ad marginem internum lineato-punctatis, externo subtus basi barbato; carpo lato, extus oblique truncato, sublævi, spina interna media obtusa, subtus antice spinis duabus obtusis; brachio brevi, lævi spinis duobus obtusis anteapicalibus, oblique positis, subtus fere nudo, spinis duabus anticis. Pedibus tertiis articulo tertio unguiculato; pedibus quintis capitulo basali brevi. Pedibus abdominalibus longis, subcontortis, longe bifidis, dente medio supero, partibus apicalibus gracilibus, spiniformibus, interna breviori, ante apicem sublatiori.

Forma II. Differt pedibus abdominalibus brevioribus, basi articulatis, apice modo bifidis, partibus apicalibus inflatis, cylindricis, dente medio supero nullo.

Vidi mares adultos similes, sed pedibus abdominalibus basi non articulatis.

Femina differt abdomine latiori, chelis angustioribus, minus punctatis, sublævibus; venter inter pedes quartos nudo, fere plano; annulo magno, transverso, fissura transversa lata, profunda, antice bituberculata.

Long. corp. 2.5; antenn. 2.6; ped. chel. 1.8.

Patria: Little Hickman, Kentucky River; Osage River.

Vidi mares utriusque formæ, ac feminas, permultos.

This species is very similar to *C. virilis* Hag., but smaller, the thorax nearly cylindrical, more flattened above; the rostrum is smaller, deeply sulcated, with the margins thickened and laterally not so sharply rectangular, but more oblique; the three apical teeth are more developed; the antennal lamina is smaller, the hands throughout are punctated and more flattened, the spines of the carpus and brachium obtuse; the ordinarily biseriated spines beneath are not at all developed, except the two anterior.

Cat. No. 213, Little Hickman, Kentucky River, Mr. A. Hyatt. Male Form I. Fem. Spec. 12.*

Cat. No. 1834, Little Hickman, Kentucky River, Mr. A. Hyatt. Male Form II., first pair of abdominal legs articulated or not articulated. Spec. 12.*

Cat. No. 271, Osage River, G. Stolley. Male. Spec. 1.

19. Cambarus propinquus *Girard.*

Cambarus propinquus Girard, Proceed. Acad. Philad., T. VI. p. 88.

Figures on Pl. I. and III.

Antennal lamina, fig. 158, *a*; epistoma, *b*; spine of the second joint of the exterior antenna, *c*.

First abdominal legs of the male:

first form, fig. 34 in front; fig. 35 variety; fig. 36 outside.

second form, fig. 37 in front; fig. 38 outside.

Mas. Rostro angustiori, elongato, subexcavato, marginibus parallelis, punctato-lineatis, apice utrinque sinuatis, spinis lateralibus perparvis fusco-corneis; acumine triangulari, acuto, latitudine rostri longiori, supra leviter carinato; cretis basalibus brevibus, margine distantibus, parallelis, vix elevatis, sulcatis, antice truncatis. Antennis corpore brevioribus, dentibus articulorum basalium brevibus acutis; antennis internis dente anteapicali infero interno acuto; lamina rostri longitudine, apicem versus latiori, margine externo sinuato, modice inflato, apice spina longiori. Epistomate antice angustiori, truncato, dimidio latiori, lateribus excisis. Pedibus maxillaribus externis intus parum villosis, subtus nudis. Thorace subovoideo, parum-punctato, lateribus subtilissime granulosis; linea profunda, subsinuata, lateribus divisa, spina laterali acuta; areola plana, paulo latiori, antice posticeque æquo dilatata. Postabdomine thorace subangustiori, fere lævi, segmentis penultimis angulo externo mutico; lamina media parte apicali breviori, subangustiori, rotundata; parte basali quadrangulari, antice utrinque bispinosa. Pedibus anticis brevibus, chela modice lata, subdepressa, punctata, subtus lævi, margine interno brevi, recto, paululum serrato; digitis fere duplo longioribus, rectis, margine interno costato-lineatis, basi intus subdentatis. Carpo lato, oblique truncato, sublævi, spina media interna, subtus spina solum externa antica valida. Brachio brevi, lævi, spinis duabus anteapicalibus oblique positis, spinis inferis biseriatis, duabus anticis exceptis subnullis. Pedibus tertiis articulo tertio unguiculato. Pedibus quintis capitulo basali cylindrico. Pedibus abdominalibus brevioribus, subcontortis, apice modo bifidis, partibus cylindricis, crassioribus, æqualibus, parte interna, apice subacuta paulo introrsus curvata, parte externa fusco-cornea, tenuiori, acuta.

Forma II. differt chela angustiori, crassiori, læviori; pedibus abdominalibus, basi articulatis (interdum non articulatis) partibus apicalibus æqualibus, parte externa non fusco cornea.

Femina differt chelis minoribus; ventre inter pedes quartos lævi, annulo obovato, subdepresso, fissura longitudinali dentata, apertura transversali nulla.

Long. corp. 2.6; long. ped. ant. 2.3.

Ordinarily, long. corp. 1.5 at 2.

Patria: Lake Oneida; Lake Superior; Niagara; Ogle County, Illinois; Delphi, Indiana; Rochester, N. Y.

I have seen many examples. In one abnormal male the third pair of legs are not hooked; some males have the third joint of the second pair of legs hooked.

A male type (Forma I.) found by Professor Baird on Grass River, St. Lawrence County, N. Y., and communicated by Professor Stimpson, is identical with the specimens from Lake Superior. Mr. Girard has seen specimens of this species from Lake Ontario, Garrison Creek, Sackett's Harbor, Four-Mile Creek, Oswego.

In one abnormal male the first pair of the abdominal legs are not developed, but they have the same shape as those of the females.

One male, Delphi, Indiana, is larger, long. corp. 3.2; ped. ant. 3.1, but very similar. The hands are more developed, as is commonly the case in old males; the abdominal legs are similar in form, but the posterior margin is a little hooked in the middle, and more emarginated before the base. The rostrum is carinated as in the type. The identity is rendered much more probable, since I have seen from the same locality male and female types, both full grown and young, and the two forms of the male. In one male, nearly full grown, the rostrum is scarcely carinated at all.

Two males, Forma I., from Rochester, N. Y., were mixed with *C. obscurus*.

The very young and small specimens much resemble those of *C. affinis*. The rostrum is more acute, the thorns at the base of the acumen long and acute, the exterior margin of the antennal lamina sinuated, but the acumen is always a little carinated, and the hands are broader and shorter.

C. propinquus Gir. differs from *C. virilis* in having its rostrum carinated and narrower, with the acumen longer than broad; the cephalothoracic carinæ more distant from the margin; the lamina of the antennæ narrower, more acute; the maxillary legs without hairs externally; the carpus below with only one anterior spine, the brachium externally smooth; the inner margin of the chela straight; the areola broader, but not so much enlarged behind; the lamina media of the postabdomen more rounded. The angle of the cephalothoracic margin behind the eyes is almost obliterated.

Cat. No. 202, Lake Superior, L. Agassiz. Male Form II. Spec. 12.*

Cat. No. 1835, Lake Superior, L. Agassiz. Male Form I. Spec. 12.*

Cat. No. 206, Lake Superior, L. Agassiz. Fem. Spec. 12.*

Cat. No. 1836, Ugle County, Ill. Male. Fem. Spec. 6.

Cat. No. 1837, locality unknown. Male Form II., first pair of abdominal legs not articulated. Spec. 3.

Cat. No. 268, Delphi, Indiana, Mr. F. C. Hill. Male. Fem. Spec. 12.*

Cat. No. 205, Niagara, L. Agassiz. Male. Fem. Spec. 12.*

Cat. No. 247, Niagara, L. Agassiz. Fem. Spec. 1.

Cat. No. 185, Niagara, L. Agassiz. Male. Fem. Spec. 12.*

Cat. No. 1838, Rochester, N. Y., Professor C. Dewey. Male. Spec. 2.

Cat. No. 1839, Lake Oneida. Male. Spec. 3.

Dry Spec., Niagara, L. Agassiz. Male. Fem. Spec. 2.

20. Cambarus obscurus *Hagen.*

Figures on Pl. I. and III.
First abdominal legs of the male.
first form, fig. 72 in front; fig. 73 outside.
second form, fig. 74 in front; fig. 75 outside.
Antennal lamina, fig. 154, *a*; epistoma, *b*; spine of the second joint of the exterior antenna, *c*.

Male. This species is very similar to *C. propinquus*, and I have seen the males from the same locality mixed in the same bottle. But having compared many full-grown individuals, I find the following differences: —

Rostro non carinato, antice plano, vix angustiori; cretis basalibus brevioribus; lamina apice acutiori, margine externo non sinuato; epistomate antice magis truncato; chela latiori, planiori, margine interno incurvo, distincte biseriatim tuberculato, linea tuberculosa alia paululum distante versus basin mediam digiti mobilis; digitis brevioribus, latioribus, externo incurvo, basi magis distantibus; carpo subtus spinis anticis distinctis; pedibus abdominalibus margine postico medio dentato; parte interna lata recta, fere carinata, apice obtusa; postabdomine laminæ mediæ parte apicali breviori.

Forma II., pedibus abdominalibus basi articulatis, margine postico non dentato; partibus magis inflatis, externa cylindrica obtusa.

Femina differt annulo apertura transversali antice bituberculata; tuberculo ventrali inter pedes secundos.

Long. corp. 3.5; antenn. 2.5; ped. antic. 2.5.

Patria: Genesee River, Rochester, N. Y.

Vidi 30 specimina.

This species is perhaps *A. fossor* Rafinesque, Amer. Monthl. Magaz., T. II. p. 42. The description is very short, and contains nothing contradictory, while the granular "gaping" toothed hand seems to designate this species rather than *C. propinquus*.

"*A. fossor*. Antennæ as long as the body, rostrum short, one-toothed on each side, a thorn behind the eyes; three pairs of spiniferous feet, hands of the first pair very large, granular-gaping-toothed, with a furrowed and bispinous wrist. Obs. Vulgar name, burrowing lobster, — communicated to me by Dr. Samuel L. Mitchell, — native of Virginia, Pennsylvania, and New York; size from four to six inches; it burrows in meadows and milldams, which it perforates and damages."

The dimensions are greater than in the specimens before me. Among the seven species known from New York, this species and *C. propinquus* are the only ones answering to Mr. Rafinesque's description. From Pennsylvania I know only *C. affinis* and *Bartonii*, from Virginia only *C. Bartonii* and *C. obesus*.

I do not know whether *C. obscurus* burrows in dams; should this peculiarity be made out, the name proposed by Mr. Rafinesque must be restored.

Cat. No. 181, Genesee River, Rochester, N. Y., Mr. H. A. Ward. Male. Fem. Spec. 12.*

Cat. No. 1840, Genesee River, Rochester, N. Y., Mr. H. A. Ward. Male Form I. Fem. Spec. 12.*

Cat. No. 1841, Genesee River, Rochester, N. Y., Mr. H. A. Ward. Male Form II. Spec. 3.

21. Cambarus rusticus *Girard.*

Cambarus rusticus Girard, Proc. Acad. Philad., T. 6, p. 88.

Figures on Pl. I. and III.
First abdominal legs of the male:
first form, fig. 80 in front; fig. 81 outside.
second form, fig. 82 in front; fig. 83 outside.
Antennal lamina, fig. 161, *a*; epistoma, *b*; spine of the second joint of the exterior antenna, *c*.

I have heretofore considered the males and females from Cincinnati, Ohio, which belong to *C. rusticus* Gir., as a variety of *C. propinquus;* the rostrum, however, is never carinated. The specimens are very closely allied to *C. placidus;* still, the apex of the abdominal legs is nearly straight, while in *C. placidus* it is slightly incurved.

They are very similar to *C. propinquus,* though the rostrum is narrower and concave on the sides, the acumen shorter, the inner margin of the hand is incurved, the interior spine of the carpus less developed, while there are two apical spines beneath, the inner one being the smaller; the brachium is more biseriated spinose beneath; the fingers are more separated at the base; the rostrum has the acumen excavated, not carinated; the external part of the abdominal legs is a little longer; the posterior margin hooked as in *C. obscurus;* in the female there is a triangular lumen in the annulus; the external parts of the two antepenultimate segments of the postabdomen are nearly rectangular.

Long. corp. 3; long. antenn. 2.6; long. ped. antic. 2.5.

Patria: Cincinnati, Ohio. I have compared a male type, Forma II., communicated by Professor W. Stimpson. I have seen nine examples, male, Formæ I. and II., and female. The abdominal legs in the Forma II. are not articulated at the base. One male from Lake Superior seems not to differ.

While this species is very near to *C. placidus,* the apical parts of the abdominal legs are shorter and more nearly straight. Nevertheless, the identity is not impossible. *C. obscurus* is very similar, but instantly separated by the truncated epistoma.

Cat. No. 285, Cincinnati, Ohio. Male. Fem. Spec. 12.*

Cat. No. 187, Lake Superior, L. Agassiz. Male Form I. Spec. 1.

22. Cambarus immunis *Hagen.*

Figures on Pl. I., III., and VIII.
First abdominal legs of the male.
first form, fig. 105 in front; fig. 106 outside.
Antennal lamina, fig. 160, *a*; epistoma, *b*; variety, *d*; spine of the second joint of the exterior antennæ, *c*.
Pl. VIII. Hand.

Mas. Rostro lato, dimidio longiori, supra excavato, lævi, basi foveola, antice vallata, dense punctata, marginibus ad acuminis apicem elevatis, vix punctato-lineatis, antice convergentibus, apice leviter sinuatis, acumine brevi, triangulari, acuto, dentibus lateralibus nullis; cretis basalibus subdivergentibus, vix elevatis, extus sulcatis, antice muticis. Antennis gracilibus, thorace paulo longioribus, articulo basali dente externo parvo acuto, articulo secundo dente perparvo; antennis internis dente medio articuli basalis infero; lamina rostro vix longiori, lata, apice subtruncata, margine externo inflato, brevi-spinoso. Epistomate lato, apice exciso (vel truncato, spina media perparva), lateribus obliquis, angulis rotundatis. Pedibus maxillaribus externis intus et subtus villosis. Thorace subcylindrico, compresso, supra fortiter punctato, lateribus lævioribus; linea profunda, sinuata, lateribus divisa, spina utrinque parva, aliaque antica ad antennas infera minori; areola plana, punctata, angusta, postice valde dilatata. Postabdomine thoracis latitudine, lævi, segmentis antepenultimis angulo externo rotundato; lamina intermedia parte apicali vix breviori, rotundata, medio subexcisa; parte basali utrinque bispina. Pedibus anticis modicis, brevioribus; chela modice lata, depressa, leviter punctata, subtus lævi, extus marginata; margine interno brevi, subrecto, tuberculato-serrato; digitis longioribus, rectis, apice corneis, incurvis, supra costatis et punctato-lineatis; digiti mobilis margine externo serrato, interno basi exciso, tuberculato; digito externo tuberculo medio et basali minoribus, basi subtus valde barbata. Carpo lato, extus valde oblique-truncato, spina interna media majori, aliisque brevioribus; subtus antice et intus multispinoso, duabus anticis majoribus. Brachio brevi, lævi, margine supero parce tuberculoso, spinis duabus parvis anteapicalibus minoribus; subtus spinis obtusis biseriatis, anticis nonnullis majoribus. Pedibus secundis intus ante apicem valde barbatis. Pedibus tertiis articulo tertio unguiculato; pedibus quintis capitulo basali annulari. Pedibus abdominalibus modicis, contortis, longe bifidis, margine postico medio subito latiori, parte interna cylindrica, apice acuta, depressa, incurva, subdilatata; parte externa paulo longiori, acuta, incurva.

Femina differt chelis minoribus, pedibus secundis minus barbatis; ventre inter pedes quartos lævi, annulo obovali, fissura denticulata, apertura magna transversa; ventre inter pedes tertios tuberculo apicali planiori.

Long. corp. 2.6; long. antenn. 1.5; ped. antic. 2.

Vidi marem (ex Alabama) paulo majorem, chelis medio magis dilatatis, digito externo intus curvo.

Patria: Lawn Ridge and Belleville, Illinois; Huntsville, Alabama.

I have not seen the second form of the male.

A female from Beaufort, N. C., is a little smaller, the antennal lamina not so broad at the tip, the areola a little narrower, the hands are very small, the moving finger has its inner margin straight, without basal excision; the example is otherwise similar to *C. immunis;* nevertheless, it possibly belongs to a different species.

C. immunis is a very interesting species; by its conical, short, and toothless rostrum it is allied to the group of *C. Bartonii*, by the abdominal legs of the male to the group of *C. affinis*. I have not seen young specimens; they, perhaps, possess lateral spines.

Cat. No. 188, Lawn Ridge, Ill., Mr. C. Ordway. Male. Fem. Spec. 5.

Cat. No. 1841, Belleville, Ill. Male. Spec. 1.

Cat. No. 301, Huntsville, Ala. Male. Spec. 1.

Cat. No. 1842, Beaufort, N. C., Mr. Bickmore. Fem. Spec. 1.

23. Cambarus extraneus *Hagen.*

Figures on Pl. I. and III.

First abdominal legs of the male:

second form, fig. 88 in front; fig. 89 outside.

Antennal lamina, fig. 156, *a*; epistoma, *b*; spine of the second joint of the exterior antenna, *c*.

Mas. Rostro lato, duplo vel triplo-longiori, lævi, excavato, marginibus punctato-lineatis, subparallelis vel subconvergentibus, utrinque ad apicem fortiter sinuatis; acumine longo, acuto, utrinque dente brevi, acuto; cretis parum elevatis, parallelis, sulcatis, spina acuta antica. Antennis validis (basis modo exstat), articulis duobus basalibus dente externo acuto, antennis internis articulo basali dente infero acuto; lamina rostri longitudine, modice lata, margine externo late inflato, apice spina acuta longiori. Epistomate brevi, lato, antice obtuso, rotundato, angulis lateralibus acutioribus; pedibus maxillaribus externis intus barbatis. Thorace leviter ovato, densius punctato-ciliato, lateribus granulosis, scabris; linea profunda, subfissa, utrinque spina valida acuta; spina antica infera ad antennarum basin; areola lata, plana, punctata, antice posticeque paulo dilatata, cephalothorace margine antico ad basin antennarum loco anguli dente parvo acuto. Postabdomine thoracis latitudine, paulo longiori, parce punctato, segmentis antepenultimis angulo laterali subrecto; lamina intermedia utrinque bispinosa, parte apicali breviori, rotundata. Pedibus anticis modicis; chela magna, lata, depressa, densius punctato-ciliata; margine interno longo, subrecto, biseriatim tuberculato-dentato; digitis validis, planis longioribus, costato-lineatis, intus dentatis, basi subtus barbatis. Carpo lato, oblique truncato, parum-punctato, spina interna media majori, aliaque basali brevi; subtus spinis duabus anticis validis. Brachio longiori, lævi, spinis duabus anteapicalibus validis, oblique positis, subtus spinis acutis biseriatis, spina ad articulationem utrinque valida. Pedibus tertiis articulo tertio unguiculato; pedibus quartis capitulo basali ovato, parvo. (Forma I. mihi invisa.)

Forma II. Pedibus abdominalibus basi articulatis, validis, brevibus, contortis; parte interna cylindrica, brevi, apice acutiori recurva; parte externa valida, antice impressa, apice compressa, dente valido recurvo, obtuso, intus duplici.

Vidi marem majorem pedibus abdominalibus non articulatis.

Femina differt abdomine latiori; ventre inter pedes quartos lævi, annulo transverso, lumine posteriori plano, sulco antico longitudinali, utrinque tuberculo rotundato.

Long. corp. 3.3; ped. antic. 2.

Habitat: Tennessee River, Georgia. The label is no doubt in part erroneous, as no portion of the Tennessee River flows through Georgia.

I have seen six specimens (three males, three females), of which the largest was a female. The males belong to Forma II., though the largest have the abdominal legs unarticulated. Apparently the males, Forma I., have larger hands and a more finished sculpture. In all the specimens the whole animal is punctuous-ciliated. The thorax is a little shorter than the abdomen.

A. affinis Say differs in having a double spine on each side of the thorax, in the very unlike forms of the abdominal legs, in the absence of the thoracic marginal spine behind the eyes, and in its larger areola. I cannot discover this species in Mr. LeConte's monograph.

It is possible that the larger female belongs to a different species; the five others are identical, the rostrum being visibly attenuated before, the acumen shorter, and the area broader. This female seems very near *C. affinis* Say. The species itself is very remarkable in having the abdominal legs formed exactly as in the group of *C. Bartoni.*

Cat. No. 175, Tennessee River, (near the borders of?) Georgia, Colonel Jones and Dr. Daniell. Male Form I. and II. Fem. Spec. 6.

III. GROUP. (Type C. Bartonii.)

The third legs of the males hooked; rostrum short, toothless; first pair of abdominal legs with the tip of the exterior part recurved, the tip of the interior part short.

This group, perhaps, unites two groups of co-ordinate value. It is, of course, possible that an examination of a greater number of specimens of *C. Carolinus* and other allied species would allow us to place them in another different group.

1. *C. Bartonii* and the allied species (except *C. Carolinus* and *C. advena*) form a very natural group. Hooks only occur in the males on the third pair of legs. The rostrum is short, broad, obtuse at the tip and toothless, even in the young animals. The antennæ are shorter than the body; their lamina is short and dilated near the tip; the spine beneath the first joint of the inner antennæ is more apical; the flagellum is short, the inner branch a little more slender, shorter, and the joints are sometimes more calcareous and fragile, similar to those of the true

Astacus. The foreborder of the cephalothorax is strongly angulated. The body, especially the postabdomen and the hands, is broader. The first pair of abdominal legs of the male has a peculiar and striking development. The tip of the exterior part forms a larger and more strongly recurved tooth; the tip of the interior part is broken, short, and conical. The second pair of legs and the third are ciliated with hairs. Burrowing habits are observed in *C. Diogenes* (united by me with *C. Bartonii*).

2. The other group, *C. Carolinus* and *C. advena*, differs in having the front border of the cephalothorax not angulated, the very narrow postabdomen, and principally in the form of the first abdominal legs, similar to those described in *C. acutus*.

Synopsis of the Species.

1st Section.

Front border of the cephalothorax angulated; first abdominal legs strongly hooked.

A. Areola linear: *C. obesus*, *C. Nebrascensis*.

B. Areola broad: *C. Bartonii* (with *C. pusillus*, *C. montanus*, *C. longulus*, *C. Diogenes*), *C. robustus*, *C. latimanus*.

Incertæ sedis: *C. Mexicanus*, *C. Cubensis*.

2d Section.

Front border of the cephalothorax straight; first abdominal legs not hooked: *C. advena*, *C. Carolinus*.

The determination of the species in this group is not so certain as in the foregoing groups. In some species the entire lack of typical specimens, or the insufficiency of materials, has perhaps misled me and occasioned errors.

This is especially the case in the species united by me with *C. Bartonii*, viz. in *C. pusillus*, *C. montanus*, *C. longulus*, and *C. Diogenes*. More ample material will either confirm my views or correct my errors.

24. Cambarus Bartonii *Fabricius*.

Astacus Bartonii Fabr., Supplem. Ent., p. 407, n. 3. — Bosc., Hist. Nat. Crust., T. II. p. 40. — Latr., Hist. Nat. Crust., T. VI. p. 240. — Say, Journ. Acad. N. Sc. Philad., T. I. p. 167, 2. — Harlan, Med. and Phys. Research., p. 230, fig. 3. — Erichson, Archiv. T. XII. p. 97, n. 17. — De-Kay, N. Y. Zoölogy, VI. 22, Pl. 8, fig. 25.

Figures on Pl. I., II., and III.

First abdominal legs of the male:
- first form, fig. 47 in front; fig. 48 outside.
- second form, fig. 49 in front; fig. 50 outside.

Inner sexual parts of the male:
- first form, fig. 135; side, fig. 136.
- second form, fig. 137; side, fig. 138.

Inner sexual parts of the female, fig. 139.

Antennal lamina, fig. 166, *a*; epistoma, *b*; spine of the second joint of the exterior antenna, *c*.

Mas. Rostro brevi, lato, fere quadrangulari, ante apicem utrinque subito sinuato, acumine latitudine rostri breviori, acuto; supra fere plano, marginibus antice ad acuminis apicem elevatis; basi foveola latiori, punctata; cretis basalibus parvis, vix rostro separatis, parallelis, extus linea punctata impressis, antice subacutis. Antennis corpore brevioribus; articulo basali dente parvo, acuto; antennis internis articulo basali spina infera antica acuta. Lamina brevi, angusta, rostro sublongiori, apice angustiori, margine externo latius inflato, apice spina longiori, acuta. Epistomate semicirculari, spina media antica; pedibus maxillaribus externis intus barbatis. Thorace subcylindrico, paulo depresso, postice subangustato, punctato, lateribus granulato; cephalothorace medio lævi; linea profunda, sinuata, spina parva infera antica ad antennarum basin; areola modica, plana, punctata, postice latiori. Postabdomine vix angustiori, punctato, segmentis antepenultimis angulis rotundatis; lamina media bispina; parte apicali æquali elliptica. Pedibus anticis brevibus, modicis; chela lata, subinflata, punctata; margine brevi dentato, interdum biseriatim tuberculato, recto, subtus sulcato; digitis validis basi non claudentibus, costatis, fortiter punctato-lineatis, dimidio longioribus, rectis, paululum subtus curvatis, intus dentatis. Brachio brevi, lævi, ante apicem supra obsolete-tuberculoso, subtus spinis biseriatis acutis. Carpo lato, oblique truncato, rarius punctato, spina media interna majori, aliaque basali minori; subtus spinis duabus anticis obtusis. Pedibus secundis densius ciliatis; pedibus tertiis articulo tertio unguiculato; pedibus quartis capitulo basali ovali. Pedibus abdominalibus brevibus, validis, contortis, subtus medio depressis, parte interna cylindrica, apice acuta, incurva; parte externa longiori, latiori, intus plana, apice dente separato, compresso, longo, incurvo, margine externo fusco-corneo, striato.

Forma II. differt chela angustiori, digitis longioribus, sæpe basi claudentibus. Pedibus abdominalibus brevibus, validis, contortis, basi articulatis, parte interna brevi, cylindrica, apice extus curvata ac subito acuminata; parte externa latiori, intus plana, apice dente magno, obtuso, recurvo, compresso, intus duplici. Variat pedibus basi non articulatis, chela perparva, digitis fere cylindricis; carpo interdum spina interna media singula.

Femina differt chelis minoribus; ventre inter pedes quartos lævi; annulo cordiformi, lumine transverso postico, sulcoque angusto antico longitudinali; abdomine latiori, summa basi angustato.

Long. corp. 2.8 – 3.6; antenn. 1.5 – 3.8; ped. antic. 2 – 2.5

Patria: Lake Superior; Lake Champlain, Burlington, Vermont (Salem Museum); Elizabethtown, Essex County, and Berkshire, Tioga County, Fishkill and Newburg (Rafinesque), N. Y.; Schooley's Mount, New Jersey; Schuylkill River, Philadelphia, and Berwick, Pennsylvania; Cincinnati, Scioto River, Columbia, Ohio; Hickman's Landing, Kentucky River; Georgetown, D. C.; Osage River, Missouri; Georgia; Greenbrier River, Virginia.

I have seen more than four hundred specimens, both very young and very old. The shape of the rostrum is variable, sometimes broader and quadrangular; the sculpture is different, the oldest individuals are most strongly tuberculated; the antennæ are shorter than the abdomen, though in one male (the largest seen by me) they are a little longer than the abdomen. The hands are variable in form, often very broad, and the fingers much separated at the base; the abdominal legs in the second form are often not articulated.

It is possible that *A. Bartonii* Fabr. belongs to this species; the description contains no contradictory characters. The description by Bosc is too short, and his figure too imperfect to afford any help. The species of Say, Harlan, Erichson, are apparently identical. DeKay's (N. Y. Fauna, T. 6, p. 20, T. 8, fig. 25) description is very brief and the figure poor, still I think the species the same. *A. affinis* M. Edwards seems to be the same (Crust. II. p. 332, n. 3). *A. Bartonii* M. Edwards is *C. affinis*. I do not know whether M. Edwards has seen the type of Bosc.

Girard gives (Proc. Acad. Philad., No. 8, T. 6, p. 88) no description of his *Bartonii*, but he quotes the works above-mentioned. Girard cites as identical *A. ciliaris* Rafinesque (Amer. Month. Mag. II. No. 3, p. 42), and this is possibly true of very large specimens.

Girard describes (l. c. p. 90, n. 13) *A. pusillus* Rafin. The description by Rafinesque (l. c. No. 4, p. 42) is too short, "the rostrum oval acute," and "wrist smooth," being the only important characters given. The comparative description by Girard is not sufficient, though the Cambridge Museum possesses one female from Lake Champlain by Professor Baird, possibly the *A. pusillus* Rafinesque.

I suppose that *C. pusillus* does not differ from *A. Bartonii*, because the examples from the North, Lake Superior, and other localities are always very small. The external lamina of the postabdomen has the inner third of the apical margin of the basal part not denticulated; in *C. obesus* it is entirely denticulated. Cilia evidently occur on the second pair of legs, and justify the name given by Rafinesque. The basal inner angle of the hand is nearly rectangular.

I have seen a female from the Mammoth Cave, Kentucky, with the eyes well developed, and a female from Georgia.

In the largest male from Ohio the antennæ are longer than the body, — a character given for *C. montanus* Girard, — but the areola is not broader.

I have compared a female type from Berwick, Pennsylvania, labelled *C. Bartonii* Er., and communicated by Professor Stimpson. The specimen is from the locality mentioned by Mr. Girard and identical with the specimens described by me from Schuylkill River.

I have also compared *Cambarus montanus* Girard, l. c. p. 88, male type from Greenbrier River, Virginia, communicated by Professor Stimpson. It is a young male of the second form, with the abdominal legs articulated. The animal is identical with *C. Bartonii*, and the shape of the epistoma forbids us to regard it as a young *C. latimanus*. The external lamina of the postabdomen has the inner third of its margin not denticulated. A dry male specimen from Virginia, *C. montanus*, Acad. Philad., is identical with the foregoing, the abdominal legs exactly resemble those of *C. Bartonii*. In the Cambridge Museum there is a jar with alcoholic specimens labelled, Isle of Pico, Azores, presented by Mrs. Dabney. It contains one *Alpheus* and three *C. Bartonii*. It seems very doubtful at present that these *Cambari* are from the Azores. The types in the Cambridge Museum of *A. Bartonii* Gibbes, mentioned in his Fauna of South Carolina, belong to *C. latimanus*. The types of *C. Bartonii* in the Mus. Acad. Philadelphia, from Pennsylvania and Pittsburg, also determined by Mr. L. R. Gibbes, are *C. affinis* Say.

A female type of *C. longulus* Gir., Proc. Acad. Philad., T. 6, p. 90, communicated by Professor Stimpson, is from the Middle States; it differs from *C. Bartonii* in having its hands smooth, very large, and apparently deformed. The fingers are small and unusually far separated at the base. In the space between them is a large bunch of hairs. I have not found such a bunch of hairs in any specimen of *C. Bartonii*; perhaps there was more room for the growth of these hairs in this deformed specimen. But I should remark that specimens of *C. Bartonii*, with the fingers about as widely separated, are destitute of any such tufts. I have sometimes found hairs in this place, but never so many in *C. latimanus*. Nevertheless, the other characters show that it must be *C. Bartonii* or a new species. I think it is *C. Bartonii*.

C. Bartonii is the most variable species; as yet I cannot find stable and constant characters for dividing them into three or four species, as Mr. Girard has done. The rostrum is often nearly quadrangular, with a little tooth in the middle of its front border, and varies in being more elongated, more attenuated before, with the angles more or less rounded and the apical tooth longer or shorter, broader or narrower. The lamina of the antennæ varies in breadth, principally in front, and in the length of the apical spine. The epistoma is often triangular, acute, often more rounded laterally, sometimes more obtuse at the tip and nearly truncated in front. The dorsal areola varies in specimens from the same locality (Cincinnati from $\frac{2}{60}$ to $\frac{8}{60}$ inches). The form of the hand is exceedingly variable, the fingers being often broadly separated at their base, frequently nearly contiguous.

The type of *C. montanus* does not differ from the typical form. The length of the antennæ quoted by Girard is variable. One male from Cincinnati, with the most quadrangular rostrum, has the antennæ even longer than the body.

I have seen more than one hundred specimens from Lake Superior,

Lake Champlain, and from the Aquarial Gardens in Boston (locality uncertain, but perhaps from the Northern Lakes), which belong undoubtedly to *C. pusillus;* still the differences given by Mr. Girard are not sufficient for separating *C. pusillus* from *C. Bartonii.*

The type of *C. longulus* is, as I think, merely an accidental variety of *C. Bartonii.* The fingers are cylindrical, very widely separated at the base, and bearded in this place and inside of the external finger, along the basal half. The shape of the finger is unusual and, I think, accidental. Broadly separated fingers are sometimes seen; the Museum possesses a specimen having the fingers on the right hand separated and those on the left hand contiguous; but I have never seen the space between the fingers bearded with hairs. The other differences quoted by Mr. Girard, and taken from the shape of the rostrum and the breadth of the areola, are not important enough to warrant a specific separation.

Mr. Say, Journ. Acad. Philad., T. 1. p. 443, says: "*A. Bartonii* has the hands differently proportioned with respect to the thumb, and more or less muricated. They are extremely common in the pine barren marshes of the Southern States, and particularly in those of Georgia and Florida." I have not seen specimens from there, but they perhaps belong to *A. latimanus.*

Cat. No. 1847, Aquarial Garden, Boston, L. Agassiz. Male Form I. and II. Fem. Spec. 12.*

Cat. No. 284, Berkshire, Tioga County, N. Y., L. Agassiz. Male Form I. and II. Fem. Spec. 12.*

Cat. No. 278, Schooley's Mount, N. Y., Mr. A. Mayor. Male. Fem., young. Spec. 8.

Cat. No. 290, Elizabethtown, N. Y., Professor Baird. Male Form II. Fem. Spec. 3.

Cat. No. 231, Lake Champlain, Professor Baird. Fem. Spec. 1.

Cat. No. 227, New Jersey, L. Agassiz. Male Form I. and II. Fem. Spec. 12.*

Cat. No. 235, Schuylkill River, Penn., L. Agassiz. Male. Fem. Spec. 12.*

Cat. No. 238, Philadelphia, Penn., Dr. Leidy. Male Form I. and II. Fem. Spec. 12.*

Cat. No. 244, Lake Superior, L. Agassiz. Male Form II. Fem. Spec. 12.*

Cat. No. 243, Cincinnati, Ohio. Male Form II. Fem. Spec. 3.

Cat. No. 267, Cincinnati, Ohio. Male Form II. Fem. Spec. 3.

Cat. No. 288, Cincinnati, Ohio, L. Agassiz. Male. Fem., young. Spec. 12.*

Cat. No. 295, Scioto River, Columbia, Ohio, Mr. J. Sullivan. Male Form II. Fem. Spec. 6.

Cat. No. 286, Mammoth Cave, Kentucky. Fem. Spec. 1.

Cat. No. 240, Hickman's Landing, Kentucky River, Mr. A. Hyatt. Fem. Spec. 1.

Cat. No. 183, Osage River, Mr. Stolley. Male Form II. Fem. Spec. 8.

Cat. No. 237, Georgetown, D. C., Lanman. Male Form II., the first pair of abdominal legs not articulated. Spec. 1.

? Cat. No. 1101, Pico, Azores, Mrs. Dabney. Male. Fem. Spec. 4. (The last locality is apparently erroneous.)

Dry spec., Niagara, L. Agassiz. Male. Spec. 1.

25. Cambarus robustus *Girard.*

Cambarus robustus Girard, Proc. Acad. Philad., T. 6, p. 90.

Antennal lamina, fig. 156, *a*; epistoma, *b*; spine of the second joint of the exterior antenna, *c*.

C. Bartonii similis, sed differt: rostro excavato, longiori, antice angustiori, acumine triangulari, rostri latitudine longiori; lamina antennarum longiori, antice latiori; articulo antennarum secundo dente externo acuto; epistomate triangulari, lateribus paulo rotundatis; thorace subovato; linea thoracica spina utrinque laterali; chela margine interno serie duplice tuberculorum serrata, digito externo supra ac subtus impresso, excavato; carpo tuberculo parvo inter spina antica et illa anteriori marginis interni.

Long. 3.2; antenn. 2.5; ped. ant. 2.

Habitat: Toronto, Humber River; Genesee River, Rochester, and Lake Regis, N. Y. Two females from Fredericksburg, Virginia (Salem Mus.).

I have seen one typical male, second form, from Toronto, in the Philadelphia Academy, and some specimens from New York, both forms of the male and female, all full grown. The abdominal legs of the male have somewhat more resemblance to those of *C. latimanus*. The rostrum and the hands, the external finger of which shows a very visible impression, separate this species from *C. Bartonii*.

C. obesus differs constantly in the linear areola. *C. latimanus* has no lateral thoracic spine, a more rounded thorax, the carpus beneath strongly tuberculated on the inner side; besides the different and more elongated rostrum, and the rounded not impressed under side of the external finger.

Cat. No. 176, Genesee River, Rochester, N. Y., Mr. H. A. Ward. Male Form. II. Fem. Spec. 12.*

Cat. No. 1176, Western New York, L. Agassiz. Male. Spec. 4.

26. Cambarus obesus *Hagen.*

Figures on Pl. I., III., and IX.
First abdominal legs of the male:
first form, fig. 39 in front; fig. 40 outside.
second form, not articulated, fig. 41 in front; fig. 42 outside.
Antennal lamina, fig. 163, *a*; epistoma, *b*; spine of the second joint of the exterior antenna, *c*.
Pl. XI. Male, first form.

Mas. Rostro lato, brevi, latitudine paululum longiori, antice angustiori, acumine brevi, late triangulari, acuto; rostro supra excavato, lævi, marginibus subito elevatis, ad acuminis apicem non interruptis; foveola basali latiori; cretis subdivergentibus, obsoletis, extus punctato-sulcatis, antice muticis postice calloso-inflatis. Antennis validis, thorace vix longioribus, articulis basalibus dente externo subnullo; antennis internis articulo basali dente medio infero parvo; lamina brevi, angusta, intus non dilatata, margine externo latius inflato, spina apicali longiori. Epistomate longitudine vix latiori, elliptico, angulis externis obtusis; pedibus maxillaribus externis intus barbatis. Thorace valido, cephalothorace supra punctis profundis rarioribus, lateribus sparsim granulosis; mesothorace compresso, supra depresso, subtilissime punctato, punctis profundis rarioribus sparsis, lateribus vix granulato; linea profunda, sinuata, antice spina ad antennarum basin infera nulla; areola nulla, linea intermedia profunda; spatio triangulari postico latiori. Postabdomine lato, segmentis anteapicalibus angulis externis rotundatis; lamina media bi-(vel tri-)spinosa, parte apicali æquali elliptica. Pedibus anticis longis, validis; chela magna, latissima, subdepressa, lævi, punctis rarioribus; margine interno brevi, incurvo, forte biseriatim tuberculato; margine externo incurvo, punctato-lineato; digitis plus duplo longioribus, latis, costatis, profunde bilineato-punctatis; interno basi intus exciso, dimidio basali extus et intus tuberculato; externo triangulari, basi forte depresso, acutiori, tuberculis majoribus basalibus internis; supra ad marginem externum dense exsculpto. Carpo lato, oblique truncato, lævi, punctis nonnullis profundis, tuberculis internis rarioribus, subantico majori; subtus lævi, spinis duabus anticis obtusis. Brachio valido; lævi, tuberculis nonnullis anteapicalibus, duabus oblique positis majoribus; subtus spinis obtusis biseriatis. Pedibus tertiis articulo tertio unguiculato; pedibus quartis capitulo basali compresso ovali, quintis subnullo. Pedibus abdominalibus brevibus, validis, contortis; intus latis, planis; parte interna breviori, apice conica, extus curvata; parte externa longiori, apice intus curvata compressa, dente lato, fusco corneo, striato, intus duplici, valde incurvo.

Forma II. Differt chelis minoribus, unguiculis parvis; pedibus abdominalibus non articulatis, parte interna conica, longiori; parte externa apice nec fusco cornea, nec striata, obtusa incurva.

Femina differt antennis brevioribus, chelis minoribus, ventre inter pedes quartos lævi, annulo transverso inflato, apertura media profunda transversali; postabdomine latiori, basi summa angustiori.

(Maxim.) Long. corp. 4.5; antenn. 2.6; ped. antic. 4.

Habitat: Evanston, Lawn Ridge, and Belleville, Illinois, and the prairies near Chicago (Philad. Acad.); Petersburg, Va.; Monticello, Miss.; Arkansas; New Orleans; Kelley's Island, Ohio; Lake Erie; Lake Michigan; Garrison Creek; Sackett's Harbor; Lake Ontario.

Vidi 16 specimina. The Salem Museum contains a full-grown male and a very young male of the second form, the abdominal legs not being articulated.

C. obesus is very similar to *C. latimanus*, but the "areola nulla" always separates them instantly. The thorax is more ovoid than in *C. latimanus*. The epistoma is not pointed anteriorly, the second joint of the external antennæ has no spine; the carinæ are posteriorly calloso-inflatæ.

One female (Garrison Creek, Philad. Acad.) was labelled *C. propinquus?* but the type of *C. propinquus*, communicated by Professor Stimpson, is a different species.

I have not seen the *C. diogenes* Girard. Although he treated of it at some length, he left it without an accurate description. The dorsal lines of the carapace are almost contiguous, so that the areola is almost wanting. I am in doubt whether it can be referred to *C. obesus*. The only specimen, from Georgetown, D. C., in the Museum is *C. Bartonii*. Perhaps *C. Diogenes* is also *C. Bartonii*.

A specimen from the District of Columbia, labelled *C. Diogenes*, in the Museum of the Philad. Acad., does not agree at all with the description of Mr. Girard, and is *C. propinquus*.

A single female from New Orleans differs in having a narrower rostrum, with the margins parallel and the tip more acute. The first pair of abdominal legs, ordinarily bearded at the margins and flattened, are singularly transformed. They are thicker, cylindrical, with the tip narrower and twisted, as is the case with the abdominal legs of *Astacus fluviatilis*. The postabdomen is narrower at the base. Possibly this specimen is a sterile female.

Another female, in shape and size similar to the foregoing (3.2 inch. long) has the rostrum broader, the margins not so much thickened as in the type, the acumen more acute. The hand is more flattened and not so strongly dotted, the inner margin more rounded, with six strong and separated teeth, giving to the specimen a very peculiar aspect. The two anterior spines of the inner margin of the carpus are long and more developed. The annulus between the fourth pair of legs has its anterior margin irregularly tuberculated. The right hand is wanting; I regard the specimen as abnormal and deformed.

Cat. No. 165, Belleville, Ill., Dr. Engelmann. Fem. Spec. 2.

Cat. No. 1461, Evanston, Ill. Male. Spec. 1.

Cat. No. 195, Lawn Ridge, Ill., Mr. A. Ordway. Fem. Spec. 1.
Cat. No. 197, Lawn Ridge, Ill., Mr. A. Ordway. Male. Fem. Spec. 6.
Cat. No. 1848, Petersburg, Va. Fem. Spec. 1.
Cat. No. 229, Arkansas, Mr. G. Stolley. Male. Spec. 1.
Cat. No. 242, New Orleans, Mr. Lawrence. Fem. Spec. 1.
Dry Spec. Lake Michigan, Professor C. Marey. Fem. Spec. 1.

27. Cambarus Nebrascensis *Girard.*

Cambarus Nebrascensis Girard, Proc. Philad. Acad. N. Sc., No. 10, T. 6, p. 91.

"Rostrum intermediate in form between that of *C. robustus* and *C. Diogenes.*" "Dorsal lines of suture of the carapace in close contiguity. Large claw nearly conical, giving to the species a very peculiar aspect."

"Fort Pierre, Nebraska; collected in 1850 by Thaddeus Culvertson." — Girard.

I have never seen any *Cambarus* agreeing with the description given by Mr. Girard, and I have not seen a typical specimen of *C. Diogenes*, the species compared with *C. Nebrascensis.* I have spoken of all the species of *Cambarus* with a linear areola under *C. maniculatus.* None of these several species agrees with the description given of *C. Nebrascensis.*

28. Cambarus latimanus *Le Conte.*

Astacus latimanus LeConte, Proc. Acad. Philad. N. Sc., T. 7, p. 402.

Figures on Pl. I. and III.
First abdominal leg of the male:
first form, fig. 43 in front; fig. 44 outside.
second form, fig. 45 in front; fig. 46 outside.
Antennal lamina, fig. 162, *a*; epistoma, *b*; spine of the second joint of the exterior antenna, *c*.

Mas. Rostro brevi, basi lato, tum sensim angustiori, fere triangulari, ante apicem leviter sinuato, acumine brevi, acuto; rostro supra excavato, basi foveolato; marginibus lineato punctatis; acumine vix marginato; cretis parvis, postice subdivergentibus, extus linea impressa, antice obtusis. Antennis gracilibus, thorace longioribus, articulis duobus basalibus dentibus externis parvis acutis; antennis internis articulo basali dente infero anteapicali parvo; lamina brevi, angusta, apice latiori, margine externo inflato, spina acuta apicali. Epistomate latiori, antice truncato, spina parva media; lateribus obliquis, angulis obtusis; pedibus maxillaribus externis intus barbatis. Thorace leviter ovato, parce punctato, lateribus granulosis vel tuberculosis; linea profunda, sinuata, spina utrinque laterali modica vel obsoleta; spina antica infera subnulla; areola modica, plana, antice paululum carinata, postice latiori. Postabdomine vix angustiori, lævi, segmentis anteapicalibus angulis externis obtusis; lamina media parte utrinque bispina, parte apicali, sublongiori, elliptica. Pedibus anticis brevibus, latis; chela lata plana, ciliato-punctata; subtus lævi, ad marginem internum sulcata; margine interno brevi, incurvo, tuberculoso-serrato; digitis duplo longioribus, latis, rectis, bicostatis, lineato-punctatis, ciliatis; digito mobili extus et basi intus tuberculato; digito externo basi intus tuberculato, extus marginato, punctato. Carpo lato, oblique truncato, parce punctato, intus subtuberculoso, spina interna media valida, interdum alia basali parva; subtus spinis duabus obtusis anticis, tertia minori interna. Brachio brevi, lævi, spinis duabus anteapicalibus oblique positis, subtus spinis biseriatis acutis. Pedibus tertiis articulo tertio unguiculato; quartis capitulo basali, ovoideo, quintis subnullo. Pedibus abdominalibus brevibus, validis, contortis; intus latis, planis; extus medio crassioribus; parte interna breviori, cylindrica, apice inflexa, conica, acumine parvo, compresso; parte externa dente longo apicali subito incurvo, extus fusco-corneo, striato.

Forma II. differt chela plerumque læviori; pedibus abdominalibus basi articulatis; parte interna apice obtusiori; parte externa dente apicali latiori, vix separato, breviori, obtuso, extus nec fusco-corneo nec striato.

Marem vidi magnum pedibus abdominalibus similibus sed basi non articulatis; chelis magnis, lævioribus, digitis angustioribus.

Femina differt abdomine latiori, basi angustato; ventre inter pedes quartos nudo; annulo transverso, modice crasso, lumine denticulato posteriori, sulco anteriori longitudinali.

(Maxim.) Long. corp. 2.9; antenn. 2.5; ped. antic. 2.3.

Habitat: Athens, Georgia; South Carolina.

Vidi specimina multa et juniora.

Juniores læviores, acumine variabili, rostro interdum longiori.

I have examined a female type in the Mus. Acad. Philad. of *C. latimanus* LeConte. It is the largest seen by me, and has the dimensions given by Mr. LeConte, long. corp. 3.3.

Cat. No. 236, Athens, Ga., Dr. J. LeConte. Male. Fem. Spec. 12.*

Cat. No. 1849, Milledgeville, Ga. Male. Spec. 1.

Dry Spec., South Carolina, Mr. L. R. Gibbes. Male. Spec. 1; labelled *A. Bartonii* Gibbes.

29. CAMBARUS MEXICANUS *Erichson.*

Cambarus Mexicanus Erichson, Wiegmann's Archiv, No. 20, T. 12 p. 99.

"CHELIS granulatis, gracilibus, subcylindricis, carpis muticis, rostro lato, apice obtusiusculo."

"Thorax somewhat compressed, always densely punctulated; cretæ prominent, divergent behind; rostrum nearly flat, broad, obtuse at the apex, with sharply recurved margins; lamina of the antennæ broad, with a little apical external spine. Hands narrow, nearly cylindrical, densely scabrous; the fingers a little shorter than the hands, thin; carpus longer than broad, scabrous, without spines on the inner side and beneath. Postabdomen nearly as broad as the thorax. The third pair of legs in the male hooked. Long. corp. nearly 2 inch. Mexico." — Erichson.

I have not seen this species. The hands resemble in shape those of *C. Nebrascensis*.

C. Montezumæ Saussure, Revue et Magas. Zool., T. 9, p. 102, and Mém. Soc. Phys. Genève, T. 14, Pl. II. fig. 22, p. 459, from the marshes of the valley of Mexico, Chapultepec, seems to be the young of *C. Mexicanus*. It is always difficult to identify or to separate species by the descriptions, but I cannot find any difference in the description given by Mr. DeSaussure. It is said that the males of *C. Montezumæ* have hooks on the second and the third pair of legs, and I have seen the same aberration in some species of this group.

30. Cambarus Cubensis *Erichson.*

Cambarus Cubensis Erichson, Wiegmann, Archiv, T. 12, p. 100, n. 21.

"Chelis granulatis, gracilibus, subcylindricis, carpis muticis, rostro lato, apice acuminato.

"Very similar to *C. Mexicanus*. Thorax punctulated; cretæ visible, a little divergent behind; rostrum nearly flat, broad, sharply notched on each side in front. Lamina of the antennæ very broad, nearly truncated before in front, with a little apical external spine. Hands shorter, narrow, nearly cylindrical, delicately scabrous; fingers slender; carpus scabrous, with sharp spines on the inner side; postabdomen nearly as broad as the thorax. The third pair of legs in the male hooked. Long. corp. 2.3 inch. Cuba." — Erichson.

I have not seen any species or specimen from Cuba. Perhaps this species belongs to the first group. The words in Erichson's description, literally "rostrum on each side notched in a sharp spine," translated by me "sharply notched," are doubtful. *C. consobrinus* Saussure, from the same locality, has the rostrum with anteapical spines. I know nothing more about these two species.

C. consobrinus Saussure, Revue et Magas. Zool., T. 9, p. 101, and Mém. Soc. Phys. Genève, T. 14, Pl. II. fig. 21, p. 458, from the marshes in the interior parts of Cuba, cannot be separated from *C. Cubensis* by the description. Apparently Mr. DeSaussure has seen the two forms of the male; this supposition would explain his remarks concerning the differences in the hands. But not having seen any specimens from Cuba, I am unable to give a definite judgment.

31. Cambarus advena *Le Conte.*

Astacus advena LeConte, Proc. Acad. Philad., T. 7, p. 402.

Figures on Pl. I., III., and VII.
First abdominal legs of the male:
first form, fig. 90 in front; fig. 91 augmented; fig. 92 outside.
Antennal lamina, fig. 164, *a*; epistoma, *b*; spine of the second joint of the exterior antenna, *c*.
Pl. VII. Male, first form.

Mas. Rostro lato, paululum longiori, fere triangulari, apice subito acuminato breviori; supra excavato, sparsim punctato, basi foveola latiori; marginibus obliquis, ad acuminis apicem non interruptis; cretis vix separatis, parum elevatis, extus obsolete sulcatis, antice obtusis, postice subdivergentibus. Antennis thorace paulo brevioribus, articulis duobus basalibus dente nullo; antennis internis articulo basali dente infero acuto medio; lamina brevi, rostri longitudine, angusta, margine externo inflato, spina apicali acuta; margine cephalothoracis angulo oculari nullo. Epistomate latiori, margine antico recto, spina media parva lateribus obliquis; pedibus maxillaribus externis intus longe barbatis. Thorace angusto, compresso-cylindrico, lævi, parce sed profunde punctato, lateribus granulis rarioribus; linea profunda, sinuata, lateribus fissa, spina antica infera ad antennarum basin; areola profunda, media fere nulla, lineari, antice posticeque profunda, triangulari, dilatata. Postabdomine angusto, lævi, lateribus parallelis, segmentis antepenultimis angulis externis subrotundatis; lamina media antice utrinque bispina, parte apicali breviori, rotundata, lamina laterali costa media usque ad marginem integra, spina marginali. Pedibus anticis modice longis validis; chela lata, inflata, parce punctata, margine externo obsolete dentato; margine interno longo, incurvo, subtus paulo sulcato, fortiter et acute serrato-dentato; margine externo obsolete dentato digitis vix longioribus, validis rectis, costatis, intus dentatis, digito mobili basi extus tuberculato. Carpo lato, oblique truncato, intus tuberculato, spina interna, subantica majori; alia minori basali (in adultis spinis nonnullis minoribus internis); subtus spinis duabus anticis obtusis; brachio modice longo, oculos superanti, lævi, margine supero tuberculato, spinis duabus anteapicalibus oblique positis acutis; subtus biseriatim spinoso; pedibus tertiis articulo tertio unguiculato; pedibus quartis capitulo basali nullo. Pedibus abdominalibus longis, gracilibus, contortis, parte interna cylindrica recta, apice acuta, longiori, extus curva; parte externa sublongiori, apice dentibus duobus fusco corneis incurvis coadunatis, lamina compressa ovali, externa recurva.

Femina differt, chelis antennisque brevioribus, abdomine lato, basi thorace fere latiori; ventre inter pedes quartos lævi; annulo transversali lumine profundo, obcordiformi.

Long. corp. 2.2 ad 2.9; antenn. 1.4; ped. antic. 1.7 ad 2.

Habitat: Charleston, S. C.; Georgia; Mobile, Ala.

I have seen male and female.

This species is remarkable for the lateral lamina of the postabdomen. In the allied species the middle rib terminates in a spine before the margin; in this species the rib ends exactly on the margin, and the spine is acute and marginal.

I have compared a female type in the Philadelphia Museum. This is the largest specimen I have seen.

It differs from the *C. Carolinus* in the short and anteriorly dilated lamina of the antennæ, with a short external spine; in the teeth of the first joint of the interior antennæ, in the anterior spine at the end of the thoracic line. In the larger specimens the hand is more sulcated beneath at the inner margin, and the carpus more spinulose.

I have seen many young specimens, but only one very young male of the second form. The abdominal legs are in their first stage of development. The tip is cylindrical, simple, and a little incurved.

Cat. No. 282, Georgia, Dr. Jones. Male. Fem. Spec. 6.

32. Cambarus Carolinus *Erichson.*

Cambarus Carolinus Erichson, Wiegm. Arch., T. 12, p. 96, n. 16.

Figures on Pl. I. and III.
First abdominal legs of the male:
first form, fig. 51 in front; fig. 52 outside.
second form, fig. 53 in front; fig. 54 outside.
Antennal lamina, fig. 165, *a*; epistoma, *b*; spine of the second joint of the exterior antenna, *c*.

Mas. Rostro longiori, lato, triangulari, antice deflexo, excavato, parce punctato, serie punctorum marginali, marginibus elevatis ad acuminis acuti apicem non interruptis; cretis parvis, sulcatis, antice muticis, subdivergentibus, postice callosis, convergentibus. Antennis gracilibus, thorace paulo longioribus, dentibus articulorum basalium nullis; lamina parva, angusta, margine externo inflato, spina apicali longiori. Epistomate lato, antice obtuso triangulari, lateribus obliquis, subsinuatis; pedibus maxillaribus externis intus barbatis. Thorace compresso, supra subdepresso, sparsim sed profunde punctato, lateribus granulosis; linea profunda, sinuata, lateribus fissa, spina antica infera nulla; areola angusta, plana, media subnulla, lineari, postice triangulari majori punctata. Postabdomine angusto, thorace sublongiori, parce punctato; segmentis antepenultimis angulis lateralibus rotundatis; lamina media utrinque bispina, parte apicali breviori, rotundata. Pedibus anticis brevibus, latis, chela brevi, lata, subinflata, paulo lanuginosa, punctata; margine interno curvato, serrato dentato, subtus sulcato; margine externo obsolete dentato; digitis fere æqualibus, validis, nec longioribus, rectis, costatis, lineato-punctatis, intus tuberculato-dentatis; digito mobili basi extus tuberculato. Carpo lato, oblique truncato, parce punctato; latere interno tuberculato-spinoso, spina media majori; subtus spinis duabus anticis modicis. Brachio brevi, margine supero spinoso, spinis duabus anticis oblique positis majoribus; subtus biseriatim spinoso. Pedibus tertiis articulo tertio unguiculato; pedibus quartis capitulo basali orbiculari. Pedibus abdominalibus gracilibus, rectis, parte interna angustiori cylindrica, apice acuta elongata; parte externa apice subinflata, dente fusco-corneo, extus striato, triangulari, compresso, acuminato.

Forma II. Pedibus abdominalibus basi non articulatis, parte interna apice crassiori, breviori; parte externa apice magis inflata, brevi, conica, subacuta, nec fusco-cornea.

Femina abdomine vix latiori, ventre inter pedes quartos nudo; annulo fere orbiculari, antice subbituberculato, lumine centrali.

Long. corp. 2.1; antenn. 1.3; ped. antic. 1.4.

Habitat: Georgia; Carolina (Erichson).

I have seen twenty specimens; the males are younger, the male Forma II. is very young; its abdominal legs are not articulated, nevertheless it has the shape commonly observed in the second form.

This species is similar to *C. advena,* but differs as follows: the rostrum is more triangular, the thorax strongly punctulated, the areola not impressed; the apical part of the median lamina is longer, the rib in the lateral lamina ends before the margin; there are no spines at the basal joints of the smaller antennæ; the carpus beneath and on the inside has numerous spines; the lateral margins of the postabdomen are not straight, but every segment is more rounded on the outside; the sexual parts differ visibly.

I think this species is the *C. Carolinus* Erich. The description seems to agree very well; the obviously small postabdomen, the more pointed lamina of the antennæ, and the linear areola are the chief characters mentioned by Erichson. The subsequent addition, that the males have only the third pair of legs hooked, places the *C. Carolinus* without doubt in this group. All the other species of the group, except *C. obesus*, are immediately seen to differ in having a larger areola, but the enlarged postabdomen separates them from the species described by Erichson.

Cat. No. 232, Charleston, S. C., Professor L. Gibbes. Male. Fem. Spec. 2.

Cat. No. 1850, Georgia. Male. Spec. 1.

Cat. No. 230, Mobile, Ala., Mr. Forbes. Male. Fem. Spec. 12.*

Cat. No. 275, Mobile, Ala., L. Agassiz. Male. Spec. 1.

Dry Spec., Georgia, L. Agassiz. Male. Spec. 1.

ASTACUS.

Corpore robusto; pedibus quintis branchiis gerentibus; antennis internis flagello breviori, inæquali; aure conico postice aperto; pedibus maris tertiis et quartis inermibus; pedibus abdominalibus maris simplicibus; femina annulo ventrali solido.

Having already given the differences of the genera *Astacus* and *Cambarus*, I need not here repeat them.

In its general form the species of *Astacus* are clumsy and oval. The fifth pair of legs has a gill, but without the broad, deeply folded membrane peculiar to the gills of all the other legs, which possess also a basal external bundle of shorter and irregularly placed gill-tubes. The inner antennæ are short, their bases thick, the joints more spherical and calcareous. The exterior antennæ are shorter than the body; their lamina is prismatic, being more thickened on the external border. The epistoma is solid, conical, a little contracted in front of the tip. The ear forms an elevated cone, rounded at the top, with a narrower circular tympanum behind. The areola is broad and slightly marked. The postabdomen is always broad, the exterior angles of the segments are often elongated and acuminated. The third and the fourth pair of legs in the males never differ from the other legs, and are never hooked. The first abdominal legs in the male form a corneous, not articulated limb, with the apical half dilated and rolled from the outside inward, forming also a channel. The shape of these legs seems not to vary in the different species, at least no difference is as yet known. In the second pair of abdominal legs the inner flagellum with the dilated basal half is rolled from the inside outward, or it has exactly the form of that of the first abdominal legs, as in the European species, or it is of a more triangular shape, similar to the *Cambarus*, as in the American species. The separated and perforated annulus ventralis behind the fourth pair of legs of the females, described in *Cambarus*, is not to be found in *Astacus*. In fact, the same part exists here, though in the European species it is never separated, but forms only a slender transverse ridge, which in the American species is curved behind like a horseshoe. In the American species it is far more dilated behind in a triangular manner, excavated beneath, and apparently more similar to *Cambarus*, but neither separated nor perforated. As yet no dimorphism of the males is known, and nothing of burrowing habits in the species. It seems striking, as already mentioned, that the species of *Astacus*, especially those from Europe, offer so many varieties, which are rarely found, considering the great number of species in the American *Cambarus*. At the same time I expressly remark, that none of the characters set forth as variable in the European species is used by me to characterize and to separate the American species.

Concerning the further division of the genus *Astacus* into groups, I am not able to give a final judgment, being entirely ignorant of the Australian species, and having before me of the Amur species but one female, and of the European species only *Astacus fluviatilis*.

The European species, or more precisely *Astacus fluviatilis*, differ from all the others in having the apical part of the intermediate lamina of the postabdomen separated from the basal half, although not so strongly as in *Cambarus;* in the American and Asiatic species this part is only more or less separated at each side, it is most so in *A. Trowbridgii*.

A. fluviatilis has a basal tooth on the exterior margin of the antennal lamina, which is never to be found in any other species. This apparently very striking character is never mentioned for *A. fluviatilis*.

The Asiatic species, *A. Dauricus*, differs in having a rostrum similar to that of *C. Bartonii*, the front border of the cephalothorax strongly angulated, a narrower and more elongated thorax, with a nearly straight, transverse suture and the above-mentioned form of the annulus ventralis.

The American species are divided according to the following characters: —

I. Margins of the rostrum denticulated; front border of the cephalothorax slightly angulated.

1. Rostrum not notched in front of the tip; cretæ visible; hands barbated: *A. Gambelii*.

2. Rostrum strongly notched before the tip; no cretæ, but two spines on each side; hands without beard: *A. nigrescens*.

II. Margins of the rostrum not denticulated; front border of the cephalothorax straight.

1. Rostrum long, margins parallel, strongly notched in front of the tip: *A. Trowbridgii*.

2. Rostrum short, tapering, slightly notched before the tip: *A. Klamathensis*.

I have not seen *A. leniusculus*, which differs from both the preceding species in the acute angles of the segments of the postabdomen.

My knowledge is too limited and fragmentary to authorize my saying more respecting the geographical distribution of the species.

1. Astacus Gambelii *Girard.*

Cambarus Gambelii Gir., Proc. Acad. N. S. Philad., T. 6, p. 90; p. 375; p. 380. — Stimpson, Proc. Boston Soc. N. H., T. 6, p. 87 (separat. p. 52).

Figures on Pl. I., III., and XI.
First abdominal leg of the male:
first form, fig. 97 in front; fig. 98 outside.
Antennal lamina, fig. 170, *a*; epistoma, *b*; spine of the second joint of the exterior antenna, *c*.
Pl. XI. Male type from California.

Mas. Pallidus obesus, rostro modico triangulari, subplano, medio calloso-carinato, marginibus subcallosis 10-dentatis, acumine parvo, acuto, recurvo; cretis brevibus, impressis, antice subacutis. Antennis modicis (apex deest); articulis duobus basalibus dente externo brevi acuto; antennis internis articulo basali dente infero anteapicali acuto; lamina valida trigona, rostri sublongiori, angusta, margine externo sinuato, crasso, apice spina acuta breviori. Epistomate parvo, acute triangulari; pedibus maxillaribus externis intus barbatis. Thorace ovato, depresso, parce punctato, læviori; linea sinuata, modice profunda; areola lata. Postabdomine thorace non latiori, lævi, segmentorum angulis externis subacutis; lamina media parte basali quadrangulari apice utrinque bispina; parte apicali breviori, rotundata, margine apicali rotundato integro (mas alter parte basali apice angustiori, utrinque unispinoso; parte apicali brevi rotundata, margine medio exciso); lamina laterali costata. Pedibus anticis validis, longis, spinulosis; chela magna, elongata, subplana, marginibus subacutis, rectis; supra ad marginem internum et externum sulcata ac densius barbata; digitis validis, rectis, conicis, chela non-longioribus. Carpo lato, truncato, intus scabro; subtus spina media antica parva. Brachio supra ante apicem spinuloso, subtus biseriatim spinuloso, spinis ad articulationem obsoletis. Pedibus abdominalibus brevibus, rectis, dimidio apicali circumvolutis, apice truncatis.

Long. corp. 3.2″; ped. antic. 3″.

Habitat: California.

I have seen two males taken by the late Dr. Gambel in California, and communicated by the Academy of Philadelphia; these same males were examined at an earlier day by Professor L. Agassiz (Proc. Acad. Philad., T. 6, p. 375).

This species is very remarkable in having tufts of fine erect hair on each side of the hands, giving to the species a very peculiar aspect. The triangular rostrum with dentated margins and the acumen only represented by a similar, but little stronger tooth, instantly separate *A. Gambelii* from the other Western species. In the second pair of abdominal legs the palpus of the penultimate joint is not longer than the leg, though this palpus in *A. nigrescens* is much longer.

Mr. Girard, l. c. p. 91, says: "Anterior pair of abdominal legs elongated resembling somewhat in shape those of *C. robustus*, to which it bears a close relationship." But the type of *C. robustus* in the Philadelphia Academy is very near *C. Bartonii*, while its abdominal legs are very different. Also *C. robustus* possesses no gills on the fifth pair of legs, and is quite unlike *A. Gambelii*.

Of the two males seen by me, one has the intermediate lamina of the postabdomen rounded at the tip, the other strongly and regularly notched. I regard the last as an accidental variety.

2. Astacus nigrescens *Stimpson.*

Astacus nigrescens Stimpson, Proc. Boston Soc. N. H., T. 6, p. 87 (Separat p. 52).

Figures on Pl. III.

Antennal lamina, fig. 168, *a*; epistoma, *b*; spine of the second joint of the exterior antenna, *c*.

Mas. Obesus, obscure olivaceus; rostro longo, valido, basi latiori, antice fere parallelo, acumine triangulari, longiori acuto, subrecurvo; supra medio canaliculato basi callo obsoleto in fovea antice angulata; marginibus calloso-inflatis, sex vel octo-dentatis; loco cretarum dentibus utrinque tribus acutis. Antennis validis, corpore brevioribus, articulis duobus basalibus dente externo acuto; antennis internis articulo basali dente infero anteapicali acuto; lamina valida trigona, rostri longitudine, modice lata, margine externo crasso, inflato, apice spina longa acuta. Epistomate lato, subtus carinato, antice triangulari; pedibus maxillaribus externis subtus spinulosis, intus barbatis. Thorace ovato, depresso, densius et fortiter punctato, lateribus granulosis; linea lata profunda, utrinque subsinuata; areola lata, plana, antice latius dilatata. Postabdomine lato, fere lævi, segmentorum angulis externis elongatis acutis; lamina media parte basali quadrangulari; apice utrinque spinis duabus validis, subrejectis; parte apicali minori, angustiori, elliptica, margine antico exciso; lamina laterali vix costata, spina media antemarginali, externaque marginali. Pedibus anticis validis, longis, corpore paulo brevioribus; chela magna, elongata, subplana, marginibus subacutis, densius punctata, margine interno fere recto, subtus paulo depresso; digitis validis, rectis, chelæ longitudine, conicis, apice spinulosis. Carpo lato, granuloso, antice truncato, subtus spina media valida. Brachio lævi, margine antico et superiori spinoso, spina apicali majori, subtus biseriatim spinuloso, spina antica aliaque utrinque ad articulationem majoribus. Pedibus abdominalibus, brevibus, rectis, dimidio apicali cylindrico circumvolutis, apice truncatis.

Femina differt ventre inter pedes quartos lævi, canaliculato; annulo bifido laminato.

(Maxim.) Long. corp. 4.6; antenn. 3; ped. antic. 4.2.

Habitat: San Francisco, California.

I have seen eight males and one female; the fifth pair of legs has branchiæ. Male and female type communicated by Professor Stimpson.

This species and *A. Gambelii* are separated from the others by the denticulated rostrum.

Cat. No. 228, San Francisco, Cal., Mr. T. G. Cary. Male. Spec. 4.

Cat. No. 1851, California, Mr. T. G. Cary. Male. Spec. 1.

3. Astacus Trowbridgii *Stimpson.*

Astacus Trowbridgii Stimpson, Proc. Boston Soc. N. H., T. 6, p. 87 (Separat. p. 53).

Figures on Pl. III. and X.

Antennal lamina, fig. 171, *a*; epistoma, *b*; spine of the second joint of the exterior antenna, *c*. Pl. X. Female type.

Fem. Obesa, olivacea, chelis obscurioribus; rostro lato longo, excavato, parce punctato, medio obsolete canaliculato, lateribus parallelis, marginatis, crassioribus; acumine triangulari, longo, angusto, acuto, fusco-corneo, spinis lateralibus validis; cretis brevioribus, antice spina rejecta; aliaque ad basin cretæ spina. Antennis corpore brevioribus modicis, articulis duobus basalibus dente externo valido; antennis internis articulo basali dente infero apicali, lamina valida, trigona rostro breviori, modice lata, margine externo crasso, apice spina longa, acuta. Epistomate triangulari; pedibus maxillaribus externis intus barbatis. Thorace ovato, antice angustiori, densius punctato, lateribus sublævibus; linea profunda, sinuata; areola lata. Postabdomine thorace latiori, apicem versus decrescente, lævi, angulis segmentorum externis rotundatis; lamina intermedia quadrangulari, apice, angustiori, utrinque spinis duabus validis, rejectis; parte apicali breviori, fere orbiculari; lamina laterali vix costata, spina media antemarginali, externaque marginali. Pedibus anticis validis, longis, corpore brevioribus; chela magna, lata, punctata subplana, marginibus subacutis, margine interdum recto subtus excavato; digitis validis, subsinuatis, chela paulo longioribus, apice spinulosis; digito mobili intus basi exciso; externo digito basi intus producto; utroque intus dentato. Carpo lato, truncato, punctato, spina antica interna acuta; subtus spina media antica. Brachio, sublævi, margine antico et superiori spinoso, spina anteapicali majori; subtus biseriatim forte spinoso, utrinque ad articulationem spina valida. Ventre inter pedes quartos lævi; annulo transverso, cylindrico.

Long. corp. 4; antenn. 3; ped. antic. 3.

Habitat: Astoria, Oregon; "near Astoria it occurs sometimes abundantly in brackish water."

I have seen two female types of Mr. Stimpson's, communicated by the Museum of the Soc. Nat. Hist. in Boston.

This species differs from *A. nigrescens* in the broad, rounded lateral angles of the abdominal segments.

4. Astacus Klamathensis *Stimpson.*

Astacus Klamathensis Stimpson, Proc. Bost. Soc. N. H., T. 6, p. 87 (Separat. p. 52). — Bate Spence. Naturalist in Vancouver's Island and Brit. America, 1866, T. 2, p. 278.

Figures on Pl. III.

Antennal lamina, fig. 169, *a*; epistoma, *b*; spine of the second joint of the exterior antenna, *c*.

Fem. Rostro longo, densius punctato, subplano, medio obsolete canaliculato, antice angustiori, utrinque marginato, acumine modico, acuto, spinis lateralibus parvis; cretis brevioribus, spina antica perparva, postica nulla. Antennis corpore brevioribus (apex deest) articulo primo dente valido, secundo subnullo; antennis internis articulo basali dente infero subapicali, lamina valida, trigona, rostro breviori, lata, margine externo crasso, apice spina brevi, acuta. Epistomate triangulari; pedibus maxillaribus externis intus barbatis. Thorace ovato, antice angustiori, densius punctato, lateribus granulosis; linea profunda, sinuata; areola lata. Postabdomine thorace latiori, apicem versus decrescente, lævi, angulis segmentorum externis rotundatis, lamina intermedia quadrangulari, apice subangustiori, utrinque spinis duabus validis rejectis; parte apicali breviori, rotundato; lamina laterali vix costata. Pedibus anticis modicis, brevibus; chela modica, punctata, subplana, marginibus subacutis, margine interno recto, subtus excavato; digitis validis, subrectis, chelæ non longioribus, apice spinulosis, non dentatis. Carpo lato, truncato, punctato, intus mutico; subtus spina media antica parva. Brachio sublævi, spina anteapicali majori, subtus biseriatim spinoso, utrinque ad articulationem spina interna valida. Ventre inter pedes quartos lævi, annulo transverso, cylindrico, bipartito.

Long. corp. 3″; ped. antic. 2.1″.

Habitat: Klamath Lake, California; in all streams east of the Cascades. Sp. Bates.

I have seen only one female type, in bad condition, communicated by Dr. W. Stimpson.

It may be distinguished from *A. Trowbridgii* by its stronger and more punctulated thorax, its tapering rostrum, with less developed spines, the shortly spined antennal lamina, the smaller hands, the carpus without internal apical spine; the annulus between the fourth pair of legs divided in the middle.

The accurate determination of this species requires the examination of more specimens; the antennal lamina on the right side is accidentally abnormal, perhaps the other is also a little changed in shape.

5. Astacus leniusculus *Dana.*

Astacus leniusculus Dana, Proc. Acad. N. H. Philad, T. 6, p. 20. — U. S. Exploring Exped. Crustac., T. 1, p. 524, t. 33, fig. 1. — Stimpson, Proc. Boston Soc. N. H., T. 6, p. 87.

"Rostrum tridentatum, dentibus acutis, medio tenuiter elongato. Carapax lævis, punctulatus, lateraliter pone rostrum utrinque bi-spinosus; areola inter suturas longitudinales postdorsales lata. Pedes antici compressi, inermes, non tuberculati, manu lævi, punctulata, carpo paulo oblongo, intus recto, inermi, apice interno acuto excepto; brachio antice denticulato, apice interno elongate acuto, dorso unispinoso. Pedes sequentes nudiusculi. Segmentum caudale parce oblongum, lateribus fere parallelis. Pedes 5[ti] branchias parvas gerentes. Hab. flumine Columbiæ," Oregoniæ. Long. 4″. — *Dana.*

In the description Mr. Dana says, "arm with anterior margin denticulate, and a longer tooth at apex, on *outer* margin, short distance from apex, unispinous."

"May be recognized by its well-developed thoracic spines, and light color. Has a general resemblance to *A. Trowbridgii;* differs from that species in having more prominent thoracic spines; the rostrum is somewhat shorter and broader, the dorsal area broader." — *Stimpson.*

Habitat: Columbia River; Puget Sound.

I have not seen this species, which seems to be very similar to *A. nigrescens*, except in the non-denticulated margin of the rostrum. The description and the figure given by Mr. Dana are not sufficient.

6. Astacus Oreganus *Randall.*

Astacus Oreganus Randall, Journ. Acad. N. S. Philad., T. 8, Pl. I., p. 138, t. 7. — Erichson, Wiegm. Arch., T. 12, p. 375. — Girard, Proc. Acad. N. S. Philad., T. 6, p. 87. — Stimpson, Proc. Boston Soc. N. H., T. 6, p. 87 (Separat. p. 55).

"Body fuscous, granulated, carpus with a sharp spine at the interior angle; arm produced into a spine on each side anteriorly; thorax behind the front with five spines, placed three before and one on each side behind the lateral ones; a large reddish spot on each side posteriorly; front little reflected on the sides, terminating in a very long, slender spine, and having a short, marginal spine on each side. Long. 4″. Columbia River.

"Testa granulata, bimaculata, fronte valde producta." — *Randall.*

Erichson, in his translation of this description, makes a mistake, "das Magenfeld an jeder Seite mit fuenf Dornen, naemlich drei vor und zwei hinter den Seitendornen"; Randall by no means says that there are five spines on each side.

"Dr. Randall's single specimen of this species was unfortunately lost by the artist employed in delineating it. No other example has been since found, although its locality has been since repeatedly searched. If the figure in the eighth volume, etc., is correct, this is a very remarkable species, differing from all others known, in possessing a median thoracic spine as well as in the length of the terminal rostral tooth, and above all in the singular lateral appendages of the abdominal segments." — *Stimpson.*

The figure published by Randall is without doubt very incorrect, giving one segment too much in the postabdomen, and a little claw at the tips of the fourth pair of legs. The curious lateral appendages to the segments of the postabdomen are probably its lateral angles, acute as in *A. nigrescens*, or the artificially protruded abdominal legs. Mr. Randall would have mentioned these very curious organs in his description if they had really existed. The tail is apparently very poorly figured, but the strong spines at the apex of the intermediate lamina are directed outward as well as in the lateral lamina and the base in the same manner as in *A. nigrescens* and *Trowbridgii*. I think the spine in the middle of the base of the beak is not at all a spine, but merely a carinated elevation very badly figured. *A. nigrescens* has a similar but not so well produced elevation; the spines could not have been very prominent, as the painter did not figure them at all. It is possible that the form of the carpus and brachium is as badly exaggerated. The exterior antennæ are apparently too short, and the length of the rostrum, so much longer than the peduncle of the antennæ, is probably erroneous; the lamina of the antennæ is figured as *triarticulate!* I think the characters quoted make it evident that the figure is without scientific value.

It is impossible to recognize this species, from an incomplete description and a very inadequate figure. The general appearance (although the mesothorax is very short) seems to point to a species near *A. leniusculus* and *Trowbridgii*, both being from the same locality, while the outwardly directed spines on the tail are truly characteristic of this group. The rostrum has the shape of *A. leniusculus*. The position of the five spines behind the front is very doubtful, and probably Erichson intended to give by the figure, which shows the little marks on each side, a more correct view of their position. The apparent incorrectness induces me to think that *A. Oreganus* can be no other than *A. leniusculus*, or else is to be struck out entirely.

ON THE GEOGRAPHICAL DISTRIBUTION.

The several different species mentioned have the following distribution: —

Genus CAMBARUS.

GROUP I.

1. C. acutus.
Louisiana: New Orleans, Milliken's Bend.
Alabama: Mobile.
South Carolina: Charleston, Summerville.
Missouri: St. Louis.
Mississippi: Kemper County.
Virginia: James River.

Var. A.
Illinois: Lawn Ridge, Basson Pudge, Evanston, Peoria, Athens.
Indiana.

Var. B.
North Carolina: Beaufort.
New Jersey: Essex.
New York.

2. C. Clarkii.
Louisiana: New Orleans.
Texas: between San Antonio and El Paso del Norto.

3. C. troglodytes.
South Carolina: Charleston.
Illinois: Lawn Ridge.
Georgia.

4. C. Blandingii.
South Carolina: Camden.

5. C. fallax.
Florida.

6. C. Lecontei.
Alabama: Mobile.
Florida: Pensacola.
North Carolina: Beaufort.
Georgia: Milledgeville.
Mississippi: Root Pond.

7. C. spiculifer.
Georgia: Athens, Roswell.

8. C. angustatus.
Georgia: Georgia inferior.

9. C. versutus.
Alabama: Mobile, Spring Hill.

10. C. maniculatus.
Georgia: Georgia inferior.

11. C. penicillatus.
South Carolina: Charleston.
Georgia.

12. C. Wiegmanni.
Mexico.

13. C. pellucidus.
Kentucky: Mammoth Cave.

GROUP II.

14. C. lancifer.
Mississippi: Root Pond.

15. C. affinis.
Pennsylvania: Delaware, near Philadelphia, Pittsburg, Carlisle, Reading, Schuylkill River, Erie.
Maryland: Havre de Grace.
District of Columbia: Potomac at Washington.
New Jersey.
New York: Niagara.

16. C. virilis.
British America: Lake Winnipeg, Saskatschavan, Red River, Lake Superior, Toronto.
Illinois: Quincy.
Iowa: Davenport.
Wisconsin: Sugar River.

Var. A.
Iowa: Davenport, Burlington.
Missouri: Osage River.
Ohio: Dayton, Miami River.
Texas.

17. C. placidus.
Illinois: Quincy.
Tennessee: Lebanon.
Texas.

18. C. juvenilis.
Kentucky: Little Hickman, Kentucky River.
Missouri: Osage River.

19. C. propinquus.
Canada: Lake Superior.

C. propinquus — *Continued.*
New York: Lake Oneida, Rochester, Niagara, Grass River, Lake Ontario, Four-Mile Creek, Oswego, Garrison Creek, Sackett's Harbor.
Illinois: Ogle County.
Indiana: Delphi.

20. C. obscurus.
New York: Genessee River, Rochester.
? Virginia: (*A. fossor* Raf.)
? Pennsylvania: (*A. fossor* Raf.)

21. C. rusticus.
Ohio: Cincinnati.
Canada: Lake Superior.

22. C. immunis.
Illinois: Belleville, Lawn Ridge.
Alabama: Huntsville.
North Carolina: Beaufort.

23. C. extraneus.
Georgia: Tennessee River.

GROUP III.

24. C. Bartonii.
Canada: Lake Superior.
Vermont: in most of the small streams in the western part of the State.
New York: Lake Champlain, Elizabethtown, Berkshire, Fishkill, Newburg, Western New York.
New Jersey: Schooley's Mountain.
Pennsylvania: Philadelphia, Schuylkill River, Berwick, Hammetstown.
Ohio: Cincinnati, Sciota River, Columbia.
Kentucky: Hickmann's Landing, Kentucky River, Mammoth Cave.
District of Columbia: Georgetown.

C. Bartonii — *Continued.*
Missouri: Osage River.
Virginia: Greenbrier River.

25. C. robustus.
Canada: Toronto, Humber River.
New York: Genessee River, Rochester, Lake Regis, Adirondack Region.
Virginia: Fredericksburg.

26. C. obesus.
Illinois: Prairie near Chicago, Evanston, Lawn Ridge.
Missouri: Belleville.
Ohio: Kelley Island, Lake Erie.
New York: Garrison Creek, Sackett's Harbor, Lake Ontario.
Arkansas.
Virginia: Petersburg.
Mississippi: Monticello.
Louisiana: New Orleans.

27. C. Nebrascensis.
Nebraska.

28. C. latimanus.
Georgia: Athens.
South Carolina.

29. C. Mexicanus.
Mexico.

30. C. Cubensis.
Cuba.

31. C. advena.
Georgia.
South Carolina: Charleston.
Alabama: Mobile.

32. C. Carolinus.
Georgia.
Carolina (or South Carolina?).

Genus ASTACUS.

33 (1). A. Gambelii.
California.

34 (2). A. nigrescens.
California: San Francisco.

35 (3). A. Trowbridgii.
Oregon: Astoria.

36 (4). A. Klamathensis.
Oregon: Lake Klameth, Cascades.

A. Klamathensis — *Continued.*
British Columbia: all streams east of the Cascades.

37 (5). A. leniusculus.
Oregon: Columbia River.
Washington Territory: Puget Sound.

38 (6). A. Oreganus.
Oregon: Columbia River.

DISTRIBUTION OF THE SPECIES OF CAMBARUS

IN EVERY STATE OR TERRITORY ACCORDING TO LOCALITIES YET ASCERTAINED.

1. MAINE. — None.

2. NEW HAMPSHIRE. — None.

3. VERMONT. — *C. Bartonii*, Burlington, Shelburne, Colchester, Chittenden County, in affluents of Lake Champlain.

4. MASSACHUSETTS. — None. I am told by Mr. S. H. Scudder that fresh-water crabs (*C. Bartonii*) have been collected in the western parts, at Williamstown. Lewis R. Gibbes cites, on the authority of Dr. Gould, *C. Bartonii* from Massachusetts.

5. CONNECTICUT. — None.

6. RHODE ISLAND. — None.

7. NEW YORK. — Seven species: *C. acutus* var. B., *C. affinis*, *C. propinquus*, *C. obscurus*, *C. Bartonii*, *C. robustus*, *C. obesus*.

C. Bartonii lives in the western part of the State, on the Hudson River and its affluents; in the southern, at Newburg and Fishkill; in the northeastern, along Lake Champlain, and particularly at Elizabethtown, Essex County; also in the Tioga affluent of the Susquehanna at Berkshire, Tioga County. Rafinesque also mentions Lake George, Saratoga, Utica, and Oswego, but perhaps the latter locality belongs to *C. proprinquus*.

C. propinquus lives in the northern part of the State, in Lake Ontario, in its affluents, the Genesee River at Rochester, Garrison Creek near Oswego, Lake Oneida, Four-Mile Creek near Sackett's Harbor, and in Grass River, a branch of the St. Lawrence River.

C. obscurus and *C. robustus* also live in the Genesee River at Rochester, *C. obesus* lives in Garrison Creek.

C. affinis lives in the western part, at Niagara. For *C. acutus* the locality is not given.

Our knowledge of the great State of New York is mostly confined to the northern and the western border. The remainder, with the exception of a small portion of the southern limits, is unknown.

8. NEW JERSEY. — Three species: *C. acutus* var. B., *C. affinis*, *C. Bartonii*. The first species is from Essex; of the second the locality is not given; the third is from Schooley's Mountain, Morris.

Of the State of New Jersey our knowledge is limited to two points in two counties very near New York, and to the rivers which empty into the outlet of the Hudson River.

9. DELAWARE. — None.

10. Pennsylvania. — Three species: *C. affinis, C. obscurus* (?), *C. Bartonii.*

The first and the third species are known from the Delaware River (Philadelphia) and from the Schuylkill River (Carlisle, Reading), from the Susquehanna and its affluents (Hummelstown, Berwick), and from the Ohio (Pittsburg). *C. obscurus* (if it be the *A. fossor* Raf.) is from Philadelphia.

In the great State of Pennsylvania, which consists of sixty-five counties, we are acquainted with only a few single localities in six counties. Of these, one is on the eastern border, another on the western, while the four others lie near together in the middle of the State.

11. Maryland. — One species: *C. affinis.*

Only one locality, Havre de Grace, at the mouth of the Susquehanna, is known.

12. Virginia. — Five species: *C. acutus, C. Bartonii, C. robustus, C. obesus,* and *C. obscurus* (if it is the *A. fossor* Raf.).

Out of one hundred and sixty-five counties our knowledge extends to only four, — the James River and its affluents, at Petersburg, the Rappahannock (Fredericksburg), and Greenbrier River in the western part.

13. District of Columbia. — One species: *C. Bartonii,* at Georgetown.

14. North Carolina. — Three species: *C. acutus* var. B., *C. Lecontei, C. immunis;* all from Beaufort, on the southeastern border.

15. South Carolina. — Seven species: *C. acutus, C. troglodytes, C. Blandingii, C. penicillatus, C. latimanus, C. advena, C. Carolinus.*

C. Blandingii is from the northern border, Wateree River; all the others are from Charleston and Summerville, on the southern border.

16. Georgia. — Ten species: *C. troglodytes, C. Lecontei, C. spiculifer, C. angustatus, C. maniculatus, C. penicillatus, C. extraneus, C. latimanus, C. advena, C. Carolinus.*

Georgia, thanks to the monograph of Mr. John LeConte, is as yet still the best explored State. He describes nine species; one, *C. fossarum,* is perhaps identical with *C. troglodytes. A. Blandingii* I have not been able to determine with certainty. Two other species have been seen by him, making in all ten species, exactly the number I have marked. It is a pity that he never gives the exact localities. *C. spiculifer, C. latimanus* are noticed as living "in Georgia superiore"; *C. troglodytes, C. fossarum, C. maniculatus, C. angustatus, C. advena,* "in Georgia inferiore"; *C. Blandingii,* "in regionibus intermediis."

Our knowledge of localities enables us to credit *C. spiculifer* and *C. latimanus* to Athens, *C. Lecontei* to Milledgeville, and *C. spiculifer* to Roswell; also to two points in the northern parts and to one in the middle of the State. *C. extraneus* is cited from the Tennessee River, Georgia, but this river does not touch the limits of Georgia.

17. FLORIDA. — Two species: *C. fallax* and *C. Lecontei.*

The only locality given is Pensacola, on the northwestern border, near Alabama. Our knowledge of Florida also is very scanty. Lewis R. Gibbes quotes *C. affinis* from Florida, but his determinations are not at all trustworthy.

18. ALABAMA. — Five species: *C. acutus, C. Lecontei, C. versutus, C. immunis, C. advena.*

C. immunis lives in Huntsville, on the northern border; all the other species occur at Mobile, in the southwestern limits of the State. Nearly the whole State remains unexplored.

19. MISSISSIPPI. — Four species: *C. acutus, C. obesus, C. Lecontei, C. lancifer.* The first from the Mobile River, Kemper County, the middle of the eastern border of the State; *C. obesus* from Monticello; the two others from Root Pond, a locality unknown to me.

20. LOUISIANA. — Three species: *C. acutus, C. Clarkii, C. obesus.*

The species are from the southeastern border from New Orleans, one also from the northeastern border, from Milliken's Bend; all from the Mississippi. Nearly the whole State remains to be explored.

21. TENNESSEE. — One species: *C. placidus,* from Lebanon, nearly in the middle of the State.

22. KENTUCKY. — Three species: *C. pellucidus, C. juvenilis, C. Bartonii.*

Besides the celebrated species from the Mammoth Cave, *C. pellucidus,* the others are from Little Hickman and Hickman's Landing, near the Kentucky River, in the middle of the State.

23. INDIANA. — Two species: *C. acutus, C. propinquus.*

Only one of the ninety-two counties gives a species; this is from Delphi, on the Wabash River, in the middle of the State.

24. OHIO. — Four species: *C. virilis, C. rusticus, C. Bartonii, C. obesus.*

Only in the southwestern part of the State, from Cincinnati and Columbia, and a little farther, from Dayton, Miami River, Montgomery County, are species noticed. *C. obesus* is from Kelley Island, Lake Erie. We know of species from only two of the eighty-eight counties.

25. MICHIGAN. — None. I am told that fresh-water crabs occur in Lake St. Clair; species are also noticed from Lake Superior.

26. WISCONSIN. — *C. virilis,* from the Sugar River. I am told that fresh-water crabs are found near Milwaukee.

27. MINNESOTA. — None. Professor Agassiz has found a species of *Cambarus* at Minnehaha Falls, above St. Paul. I have not seen the specimen.

28. IOWA. — One species: *C. virilis* is found in the Mississippi at Davenport and Burlington, along the southeastern border. The State is unexplored.

29. ILLINOIS. — Seven species: *C. acutus* var. A., *C. troglodytes, C. virilis, C. placidus, C. propinquus, C. immunis, C. obesus.*

This State is one of the best explored, for I have seen in the Museum of the Chicago Academy sixty glasses with *Cambarus*, mostly from the different localities of Illinois, but I was not able to ascertain the species. There are known from the northern border, as at Chicago and Evanston, *C. acutus* var. A., and *C. obesus*; from the middle northern parts (Illinois River and affluents), Ogle County, Lawn Ridge, Basson Pudge, Peoria, Athens, *C. acutus* var. A., *C. troglodytes*, *C. propinquus*, *C. immunis*, *C. obesus*, and from the western border from the Mississippi, from Quincy and Belleville, *C. virilis*, *C. placidus*, and *C. immunis*.

30. Missouri. — Five species: *C. acutus*, *C. virilis*, *C. juvenilis*, *C. Bartonii*, *C. obesus*. All are from St. Louis and from the Osage River, near the centre of the State.

31. Arkansas. — One species: *C. obesus*, locality unknown.

32. Texas. — Three species: *C. Clarkii*, *C. virilis*, *C. placidus*; the first occurs near the middle of the State, between San Antonio and El Paso del Norte; of the others the localities are unknown.

33. Indian Territory. — None.

34. Kansas. — None. I have seen only one species in the Chicago Museum.

35. Nebraska. — One species: *C. Nebrascensis*, without locality.

36. Dakota. — None. I have seen only one specimen in the Chicago Museum.

37. Wyoming. — None.

38. Montana. — None.

39. Idaho. — None.

40. Colorado. — None.

41. Utah. — None.

42. Arizona. — None.

43. New Mexico. — None.

44. Nevada. — None.

45. Washington Territory. — One species: *A. leniusculus*, at Puget Sound.

46. Oregon. — Three species: *A. Trowbridgii*, *A. leniusculus*, *A. Klamathensis*. From Astoria, from the Columbia River and Lake Klamath. The locality of *A. Oreganus* is doubtful.

47. California. — Two species: *A. Gambelii* and *A. nigrescens*. From San Francisco.

British America. — Five species: *C. virilis*, *C. propinquus*, *C. Bartonii*, *C. robustus*, *C. Klamathensis*.

In Canada from the Humber River near Toronto is noticed *C. robustus*. In Lake Superior *C. Bartonii*, *C. propinquus*, *C. virilis* occur, the latter also in Lake Winnipeg, Saskatschavan, and the Red River. *A. Klamathensis* is found in British Columbia.

Mexico. — Two species: *C. Wiegmanni*, *C. Mexicanus*. One from the marshes of the valley of Mexico, the other without known locality.

Cuba. — One species: *C. Cubensis*, from the marshes in the central part of Cuba.

According to the list given above, we know nothing upon the geographical distribution or even the existence of species in the following nineteen States and Territories: —

1. Maine, New Hampshire, Massachusetts, Connecticut, Rhode Island, Delaware, Michigan, Minnesota, Indian Territory, Kansas, Dakota, Wyoming, Montana, Idaho, Colorado, Utah, Arizona, New Mexico, Nevada.
2. From nine States and Territories we know one species, the locality being definitely known in only one half of them, viz., Vermont, Maryland, District of Columbia, Tennessee, Iowa, Arkansas, Wisconsin, Nebraska, and Washington Territory.
3. From three States we know two species, viz., Florida, Indiana, California.
4. From eight States we know three species, viz., New Jersey, Pennsylvania, North Carolina, Louisiana, Kentucky, Texas, Oregon.
5. From Ohio and Mississippi, four species.
6. From three States we know five species, viz., Virginia, Alabama, Missouri.
7. From three States we know seven species, viz., New York, Illinois, South Carolina.
8. From one State we know ten species, viz., Georgia.

The first step to take, and the best way if we would make progress in knowledge, is always to ascertain how limited it is; and for this purpose it is evidently profitable to show that the undoubtedly unrivalled materials before me represent a very limited part of the gigantic territory comprised in the United States. Besides more than the western half, noticed before as not represented in our catalogue, it is surprising that the much-explored New England States are nearly wanting. Perhaps the multitude of manufactories and the consequent spoiling of the water, especially of the running streams, has some influence on the rarity of the fresh-water crabs; but a more careful exploration is doubtless necessary to prove the existence or the absence of *Astacidæ*.

At the same time some of the other States, seemingly better represented in our catalogue, are far from being well explored; even some, furnishing the largest number of species, are in reality to a great extent unexplored.

Of the great State of New York we are only acquainted with the eastern border, and in New Jersey with a single locality in the vicinity of New York City. In Maryland and the two Carolinas we know only a small area, along the eastern limits. In Florida, Alabama, and Louisiana, only the localities very near to each other are noticed, while all the rest of these States are unexplored. The number of species in

Georgia, the best explored portion of the country, suggests how much may be found in the adjacent States. The Middle States are in parts better explored, but without doubt they will furnish many new species or show a wider distribution of the known species, as is stated in our catalogue.

It would be very interesting to ascertain whether the extensive table-lands between the Sierra Nevada of California and the Rocky Mountains, as well as the great American desert, possess species of the genus *Astacus* or of the genus *Cambarus* or not. As yet nothing is known about these regions.

Perhaps under these circumstances a detailed exposition of the geographical distribution of the North American *Astacidæ* would be premature and incorrect, but some facts are too striking and too apparent to be overlooked, even at this stage of our knowledge.

The first and chief point ascertained as yet is the strict limitation of the genera *Astacus* and *Cambarus*, which completely exclude each other. In the parts west of the Sierra Nevada, and perhaps of the Rocky Mountains, lives the genus *Astacus*, in all the eastern parts the genus *Cambarus*. At present no exception is known. This fact is all the more interesting, as the only species known from the eastern parts of Asia, *Astacus Dauricus Pallas*, which is probably identical with *Astacus leptorhinus* Fisher, from the Amur River, seems to be a group intermediate between the European and North American species of *Astacus*, and more nearly related to the species of the latter country.

Our knowledge of the geographical distribution of the North American species of *Astacus* is as yet too limited for us to say anything more respecting them.

The second fact, which seems to be ascertained, is that the genus *Cambarus* is confined to the other parts of North America and perhaps to the Antilles. I have not seen the species described by Erichson and de Saussure from Cuba, but it doubtless belongs to the genus *Cambarus*. The asserted presence of the genus *Cambarus* in South America is to be discredited, unless further and more trustworthy evidence be produced in its favor. *C. Chilensis*, mentioned by Erichson as a species of *Cambarus*, was never seen by him, and seems from the description to be more nearly related to *Cheraps*, or perhaps to represent some distinct genus. I have seen one and only one specimen of *Astacidæ* from Brazil, — if there be no error as to the habit, which was apparently the case with some *Astacus fluviatilis* communicated to me as Brazilian species, — a male in a very bad state of preservation, and evidently nearly related to *C. Chilensis*. As the specimen is dry and very old, it is impossible to ascertain whether it have gills or not on the fifth pair of legs.

The *C. Bartonii*, figured and described as perhaps from Brazil by Mr. Dana in his excellent work, is certainly not identical with the *C. Bar-*

tonii from North America. The habitat is uncertain, and so not of decisive value.*

Concerning the geographical distribution of the genus *Cambarus*, we find the interesting fact that the most distinct group, containing the species related to *C. acutus*, seems to be confined to a limited territory. Its boundaries answer for the most part to the Southern fauna, traced by Professor L. Agassiz for the *Chelonians*, but is somewhat more extensive, as some species are observed to live also in the upper parts of the rivers and their affluents. Beginning on the Atlantic coast in Virginia (also farther north, as with the *Chelonians*), it extends through the Carolinas, Georgia, Florida, Alabama, Mississippi, Louisiana, and Texas.

Some species follow up the Mississippi and its tributaries for a great distance, while a peculiar variety, described by me as *C. acutus* var. A, has its habitat far to the north, and is not to be found in the southern parts. It is very interesting to remark that the same species is to be found farther north on the Atlantic coast, forming also a peculiar variety, described by me as *C. acutus* var. B, from New Jersey and New York. It was impossible for me to give an adequate account of it, as I have not seen the male.

Our knowledge of the Mexican fauna is very meagre, but it seems probable that a few species at least belong to the same group. Still more interesting is the fact that some species of the other *Cambarus* groups, living within the limits noticed for the species for the first group, have an analogous appearance and shape of body, viz., *C. lancifer*, *C. immunis*, *C. extraneus*, *C. advena*, and *C. Carolinus*.

I have heretofore stated that these species, even when viewed under other relations, constitute aberrant forms. But it should be remembered that several species, viz., *C. placidus*, *C. obesus*, *C. latimanus*, which also live in the same southern country, belong in all their characters to very different groups. The groups of *Cambarus*, as defined by me, do not apparently coincide with certain faunal regions.

The species of the second group, except the aberrant forms before mentioned, especially the species related to *C. virilis*, belong to the northern and middle parts of North America. These species occur especially in the Northern Lakes and their affluents, also in the Missouri, Mississippi, Ohio, and their tributaries, and in Texas.

C. affinis, a somewhat peculiar species, alone lives in the rivers running eastward to the Atlantic coast, in the Hudson, Delaware, Potomac, Susquehanna, and their affluents.

* Von Martens, in Troschel Archiv, 1869, T. 35, p. 15 sqq., describes two species of fresh-water crabs from Brazil, *Astacus pilimanus*, p. 15, Tab. 2, fig. 1, from Porto Allegre and Santa Cruz, in the affluents of the Rio Pardo River, which is an affluent of the Jacuhy River, with burrowing habits, *Astacus Brasiliensis*, p. 16, Tab. 2, fig. 2, from Porto Alegre and from Roedersberg, in ponds and small rivers. The latter is perhaps the species from Brazil mentioned by me, p. 11.

Professor H. Burmeister writes to me that he has seen a species of *Astacus* from the Banda oriental.

Evidently the faunal area of the second group of species coincides with that of the first group in the vast regions watered by the Mississippi and its branches, without touching, except in some aberrant forms, the southeastern regions.

The third group occurs in the whole country inhabited by the two others, in the Northern Lakes and their affluents, in the rivers running both to the Atlantic coast and to the Mississippi; in short, equally in the northern and southern, in the eastern and western parts of the United States. *C. Bartonii* and the next allied species are to be found in Lake Superior and in the St. Lawrence River, in Nebraska, Arkansas, Louisiana, and along the Atlantic coast from Vermont to South Carolina, and perhaps to Florida.

An interesting fact in the geographical distribution of the animals is the association or exclusion of certain species, also the representation of given species in different localities by others that are closely allied.

Concerning the association of particular species, I would remark that the materials before me give for two localities four species. I have seen from Charleston, *C. acutus*, *C. troglodytes*, *C. penicillatus*, and *C. advena;* from Mobile, *C. acutus*, *C. Lecontei*, *C. versutus*, and *C. advena.*

From six localities three species are cited: from New Orleans, *C. acutus*, *C. Clarkii*, *C. obesus;* Lawn Ridge, *C. acutus*, *C. immunis*, *C. obesus;* Beaufort, *C. acutus*, *C. Lecontei*, *C. immunis;* Lake Superior, *C. virilis*, *C. propinquus*, *C. Bartonii;* Rochester, *C. propinquus*, *C. obscurus*, *C. robustus;* Osage River, *C. virilis*, *C. juvenilis*, *C. Bartonii.*

Two species are quoted from more localities: from St. Louis, *C. acutus*, *C. obesus;* Root Pond, *C. Lecontei*, *C. lancifer;* Athens, Ga., *C. spiculifer*, *C. latimanus;* Quincy, Ill., *C. virilis*, *C. placidus;* Niagara, *C. affinis*, *C. propinquus;* Philadelphia, *C. affinis*, *C. Bartonii;* the Mammoth Cave, *C. pelulcidus*, *C. Bartonii;* Cincinnati, *C. rusticus*, *C. Bartonii;* Evanston, Ill., *C. acutus*, *C. obesus.*

The list given shows no regularity, at least I am not able to find any; still, this is perhaps because of the incompleteness of the material. Looking over the species that occur together, we find the most nearly related living with those that are evidently different; those of the first group with others of the second, some of the second with others of the third, and even all three groups in the same locality.

No more regularity is to be found in association of the different species. *C. acutus* lives in seven different localities together with eight different species, the half belonging to the other groups. *C. advena* is found in the same localities with five other species, none belonging to its own group. *C. Lecontei*, *C. obesus*, *C. virilis*, *C. Bartonii* live together with four, *C. propinquus* with five different species, partly belonging to different groups.

The uncertainty already referred to prevents my dwelling upon the exclusion or representation of particular species. New explorations would no doubt very soon and perhaps entirely alter any views we might form from incomplete materials.

C. acutus, *C. virilis*, *C. Bartonii*, and *C. obesus* are the most widely spread species.

The geographical distribution according to the river systems is as follows: —

The rivers west of the Mississippi, running to the Gulf of Mexico, are little explored. From Texas, perhaps from the branches of the Colorado, *C. Clarkii*, *C. virilis*, and *C. placidus* are cited; the two latter were collected by Mr. Stolley, the locality not being given.

The Mississippi and its numerous well-known affluents contain a great number of species. In the lower part of this river, and in its inferior affluents, especially near its mouth, as at New Orleans, occur *C. acutus*, *C. Clarkii*, *C. obesus;* a little higher up in the branches on either side are found *C. Clarkii*, *C. Lecontei*, *C. lancifer*, *C. obesus*.

The Ohio River and its affluents furnish *C. virilis*, *C. placidus*, *C. juvenilis*, *C. rusticus*, *C. Bartonii;* while in the Wabash River, one of its lower branches, occur *C. acutus* and *C. propinquus*. The fauna of the Ohio River is also quite different from that of the Lower Mississippi, if we exclude from consideration *C. acutus* and the two species *C. virilis* and *C. placidus*, which are found in the Colorado River.

The middle part of the Mississippi, the Missouri, with the Osage River and their several branches, contain *C. acutus*, *C. obesus*, *C. Nebrascensis*, *C. placidus*, *C. virilis*, *C. juvenilis*, *C. Bartonii;* the three latter species being from the Osage River; also nearly the same species as are cited in the Ohio fauna.

In the Upper Mississippi and its affluents, especially in the Illinois River, are found *C. acutus* var. A., *C. troglodytes*, *C. virilis*, *C. placidus*, *C. propinquus*, *C. immunis*, *C. obesus*. It is worthy of remark that a channel unites the Illinois and the Chicago Rivers, and that perhaps in this way may be explained the occurrence of the southern species *C. acutus* and *C. obesus* at Evanston, on Lake Michigan. Among the several rivers and their branches lying to the east of the Mississippi, it may be added that the Mobile River contains *C. Clarkii*, *C. Lecontei*, *C. versutus*, *C. immunis;* while in the Florida rivers occur *C. Lecontei* and *C. fallax*. Two of them, *C. versutus* and *C. fallax*, are not as yet known farther to the west.

The rivers east of the Alleghany Mountains furnish in Georgia, *C. troglodytes*, *C. Lecontei*, *C. spiculifer*, *C. angustatus*, *C. maniculatus*, *C. penicillatus*, *C. extraneus*, *C. latimanus*, *C. advena*, *C. Carolinus;* also besides the first two a quite different and new fauna. Farther north, in South Carolina, live *C. acutus*, *C. troglodytes*, *C. Blandingii*, and *C. penicillatus;* in North Carolina, *C. acutus*, *C. Lecontei*, and *C. immunis*, — species which are nearly all, except *C. Blandingii* and the Georgian *C. penicillatus*, represented at the mouth of the Mississippi.

In Virginia, in the James River and its affluents, we find *C. Bartonii* and *C. robustus*, with the southern form *C. acutus*. The first-named species descends no farther than to the middle of the Mississippi; the second is of a decidedly northeastern type, more properly belonging to the fauna characteristic of the waters that empty into the St. Lawrence. In the more northern rivers, especially in the Potomac, Susquehanna, Delaware, and their tributaries, we find *C. Bartonii* and *C. affinis*, and perhaps *C. obscurus*.

In the Hudson River, also in the other streams as far north as Vermont, and in Lake Champlain, occurs *C. Bartonii*. But the mouth of the Hudson River in New Jersey and New York is the extreme limit of a peculiar variety of the southern species *C. acutus*, which is well represented in North Carolina.

The fauna east of the Alleghany Mountains is also very peculiar. Perhaps the most peculiar part is the well-explored and striking fauna of Georgia. But we find farther to the north — besides *C. acutus*, widely extended in the South, and *C. Bartonii*, a species to be found in the whole middle part of the United States, — the exclusively northeastern species *C. affinis* and *C. obscurus*.

The northern fauna, comprised in the immense water-basin of the St. Lawrence and its tributaries, furnishes in Lake Superior, *C. virilis*, *C. propinquus*, *C. rusticus*, *C. Bartonii*; in the Niagara, *C. affinis* and *C. propinquus*; in Lake Ontario and its affluents, especially Genesee River and Lake Oneida, *C. propinquus*, *C. obscurus*, *C. Bartonii*, *C. robustus*, *C. obesus*. Some of these species, and in fact all those found in Lake Superior, as *C. virilis*, *C. propinquus*, *C. rusticus*, *C. Bartonii*, *C. obesus*, are also represented in the regions watered by the Upper Mississippi and its branches; *C. obscurus*, *C. affinis*, and *C. robustus* are the only species peculiar to the northern fauna. The remarkable habitat of *C. acutus* and *C. obesus* in Lake Michigan has been before mentioned.

C. virilis occurs in the more northern waters, which empty into Hudson's Bay, especially in Lake Winnipeg, Saskatschavan, and Red River. I am told that these waters are connected in the summer time through marshes with the affluents of the Upper Mississippi.

We also find true, especially for the genus *Cambarus*, that the United States are divided into three great faunal regions, — the region traversed by the Mississippi; the eastern region, lying between the Alleghany Mountains and the Atlantic coast; and the northern region, which is watered by the Northern Lakes and the St. Lawrence. I have not spoken of the Mexican and Cuban species, my acquaintance with them being as yet very imperfect.

The three great regions just mentioned, particularly the first and the second, doubtless comprise several subordinate faunal districts. The region watered by the Mississippi apparently divides itself into two parts, a southern and a northern, the latter beginning near the mouth of the Ohio River. The eastern region has a decided and peculiar southern fauna, which is perhaps to be united with that of Cuba, and a northern fauna beginning in Pennsylvania. In the northern region there seems hardly any difference between the eastern and western parts. Nevertheless, it is certain that some species belong to more than one region, and that these regions do not coincide with the three principal groups of the genus *Cambarus*. The first group, as has been already stated, prevails in the southern parts of the western and eastern faunal region; the second group prevails partly in the northern part of the eastern faunal region.

The examination of the distribution of single species, or rather the exact determination of the circle in which every species lives and the central point which is to be taken as its most proper habitat, would be very interesting, if the materials at command were sufficiently abundant. The greatest impediment to such an examination is the scantiness of our knowledge, I may say our almost entire ignorance, of the great country comprising the Alleghany Mountains and circumjacent regions.

A detailed examination of the questions suggested being as yet impossible, I may be permitted to offer a few words upon some of the most widely spread species.

The central point of *C. acutus* seems to be the southern shore around the mouth of the Mississippi; of *C. affinis*, the Lower Potomac; of *C. virilis*, Lake Superior; of *C. propinquus*, Lake Ontario; of *C. obesus*, the middle part of the Mississippi; of *C. Bartonii*, perhaps the middle of the eastern part of the United States. Some of these so-called central points are in fact not at all central, they being either near the shore of the sea or not far from the limits, so far as we yet know, of the distribution of the species. I accordingly attach no great value to them, as they are liable very soon to be greatly modified by new explorations.

The number of species now known to belong to the old genus *Astacus* is 56. Of these there are in America, 40 (two in South America); New Holland, 11; Asia, 2; Europe, 2; Africa, 1.

As now distributed, there belong to the genus *Cambarus*, 32; *Astacus*, 13; (Astacoides) *Astacoides*, 4; *Cheraps*, 1; *Engæus*, 2. The systematic position of the other species is not yet ascertained.

INDEX.

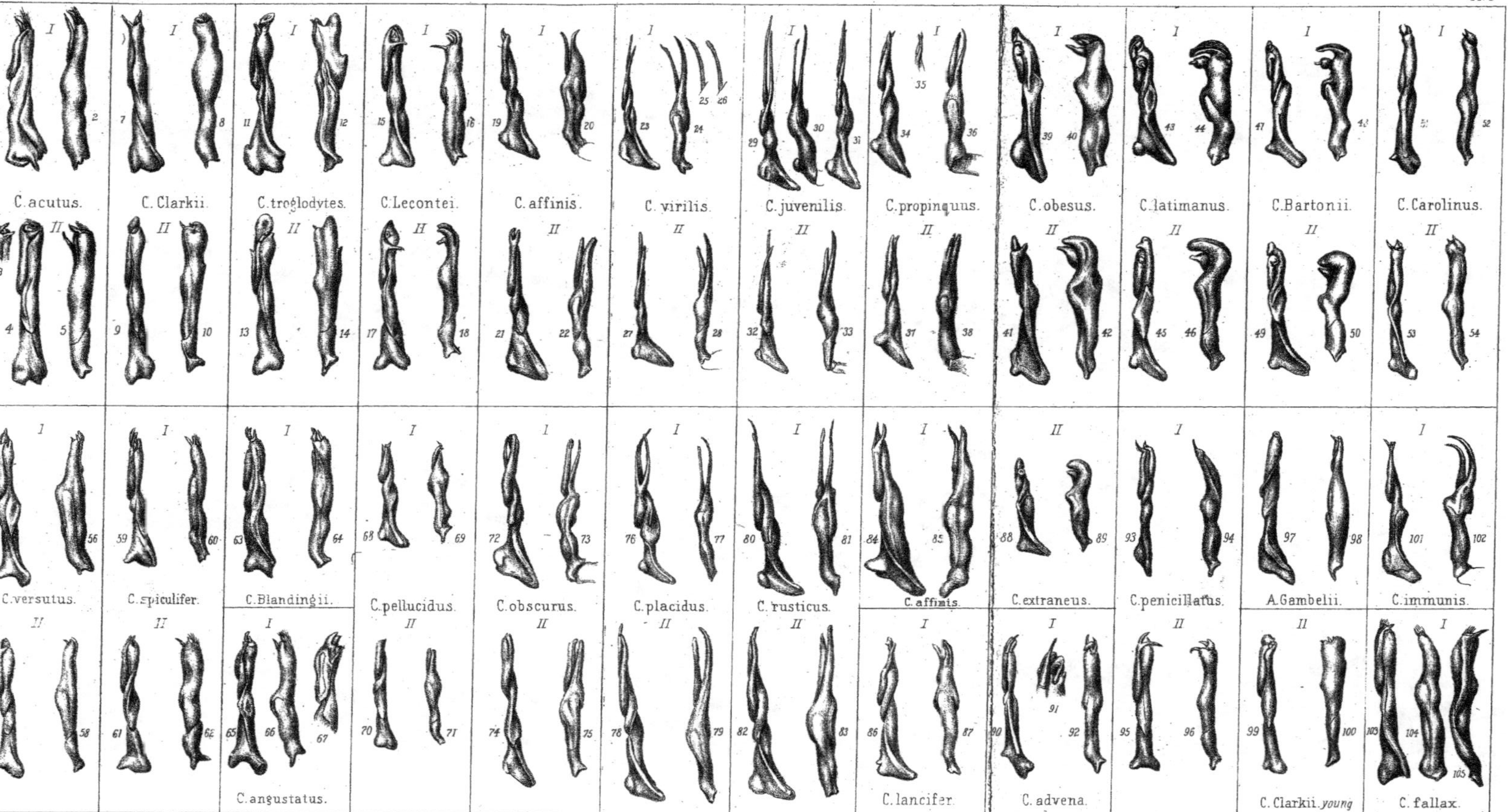

Dr. Hagen del. — C. Roetter on stone

New Eng. Lith. Co. Boston.

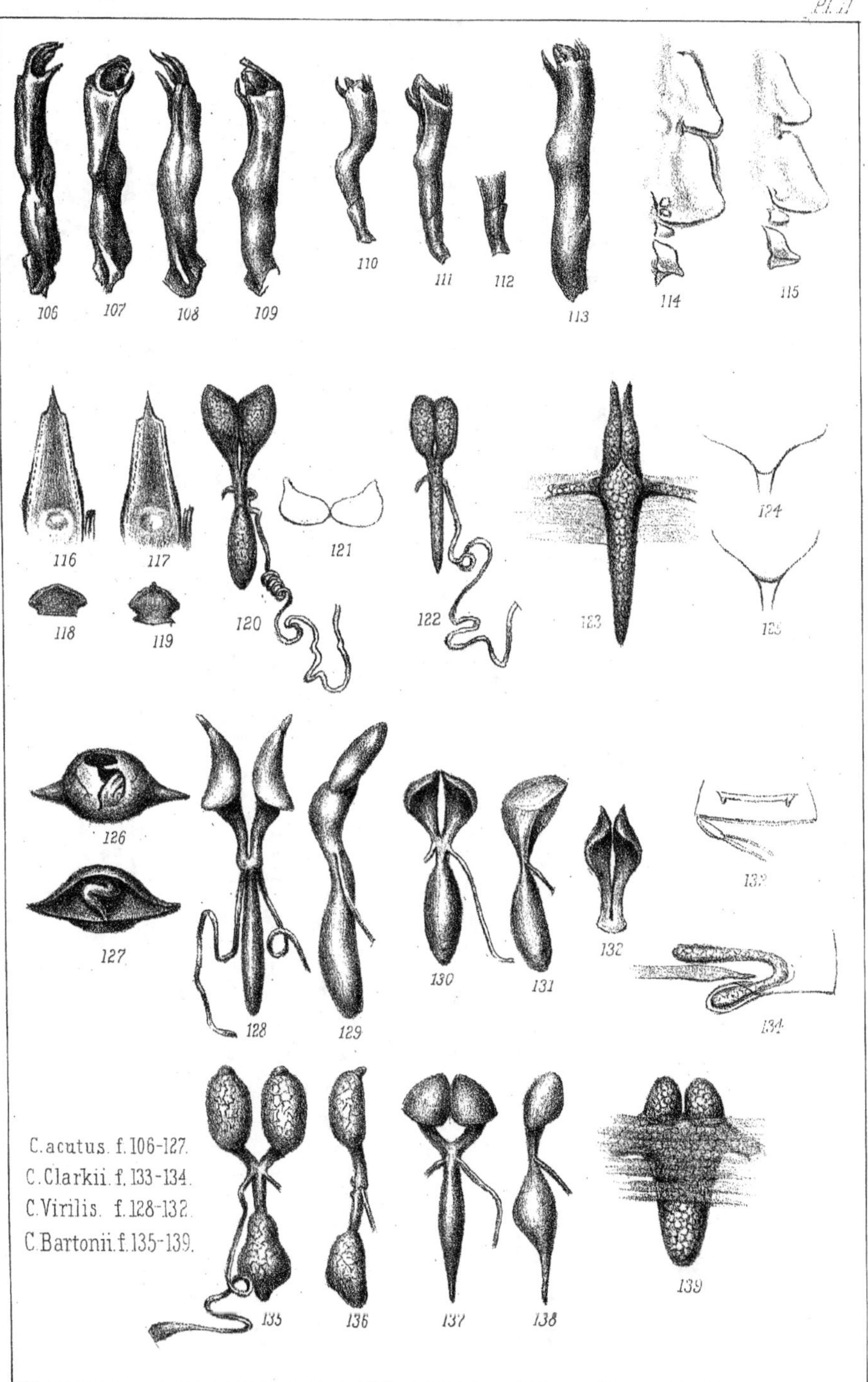

Dr. Hagen, del.- P. Roetter, on stone. New Eng. Lith. Co. Boston.

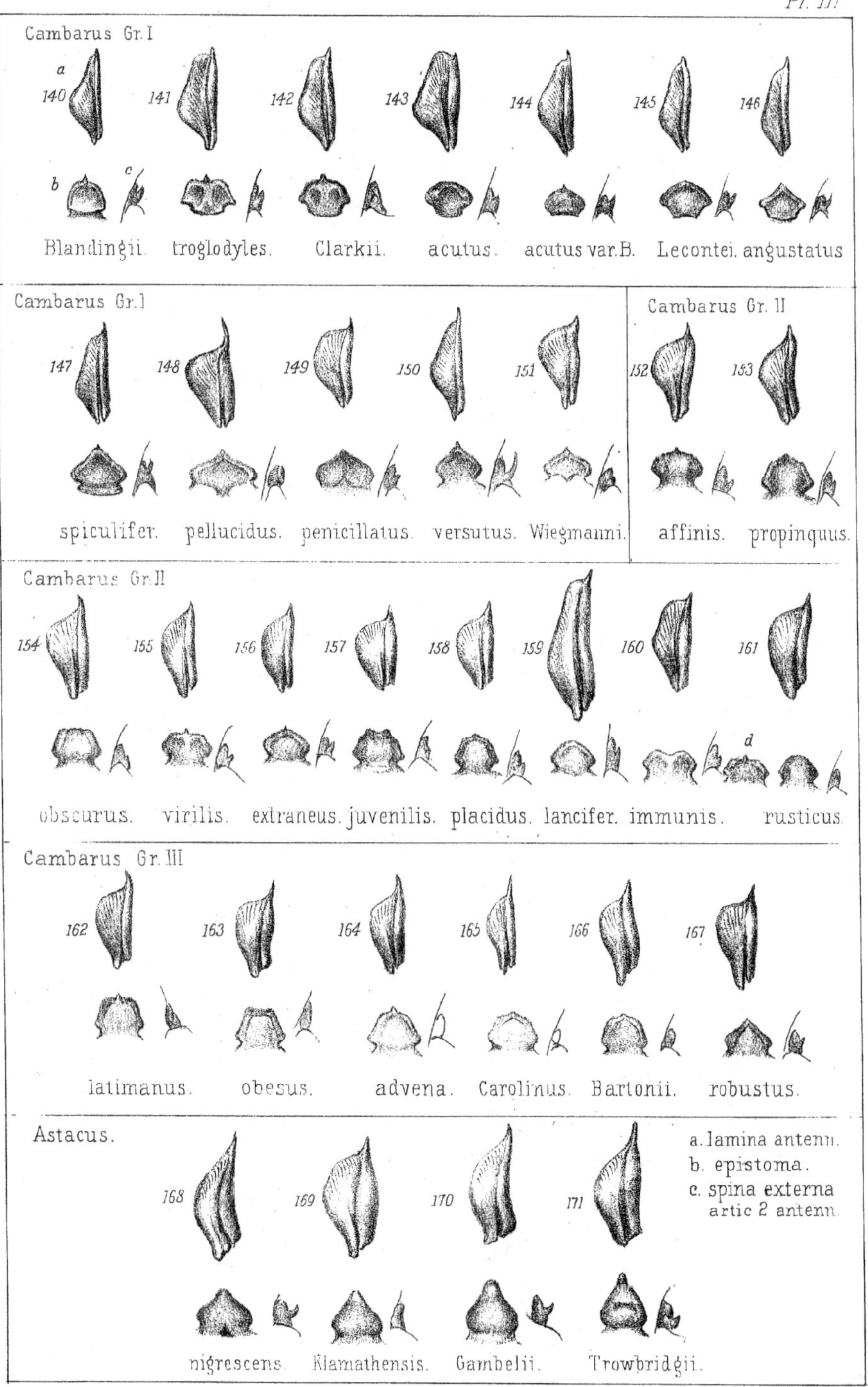

Dr. Hagen, del. – P. Roetter, on stone.

New Eng. Lith. Co. Boston.

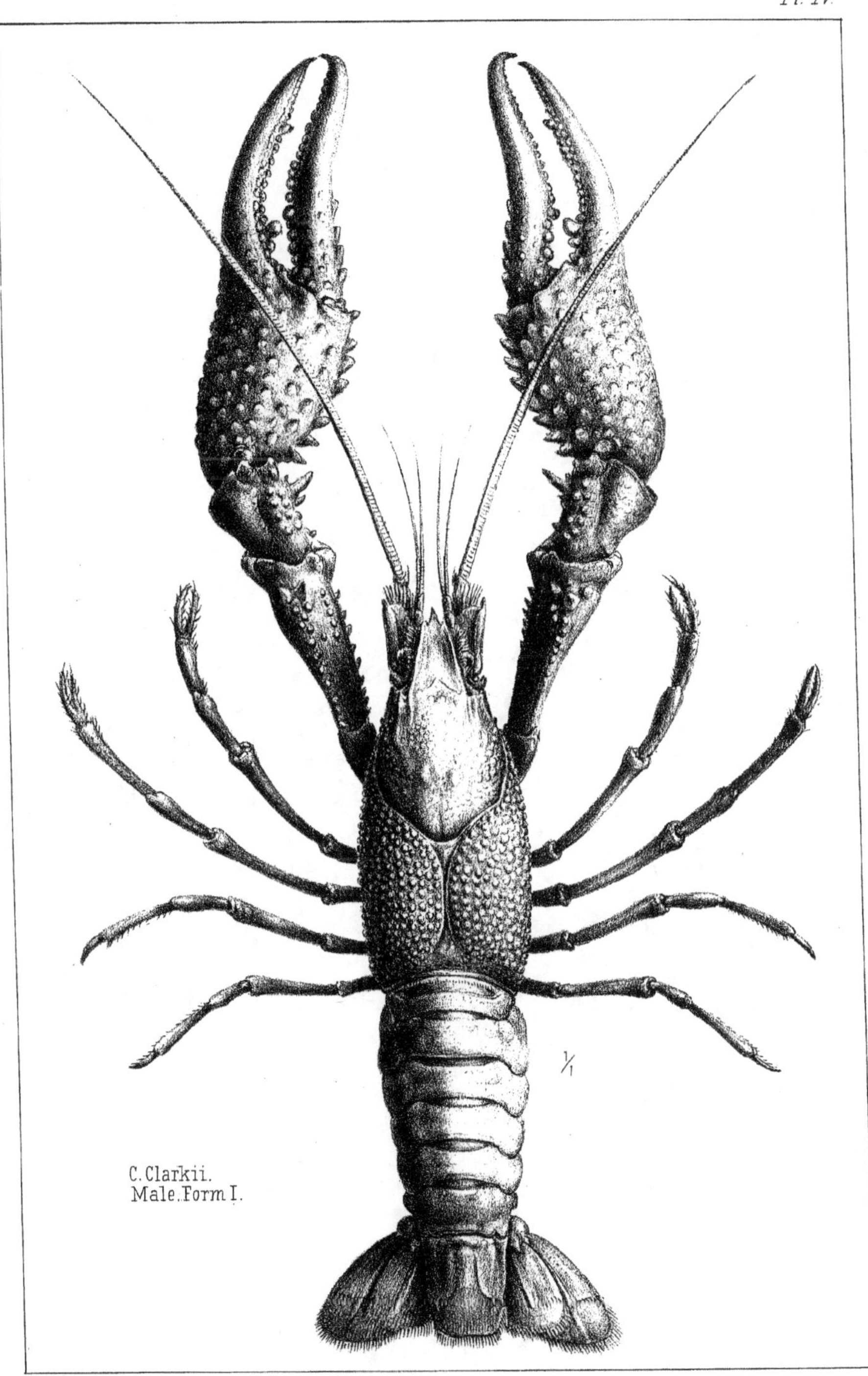

C. Clarkii.
Male. Form I.

P. Roetter, on stone from nat.

New Eng. Lith. Co. Boston.

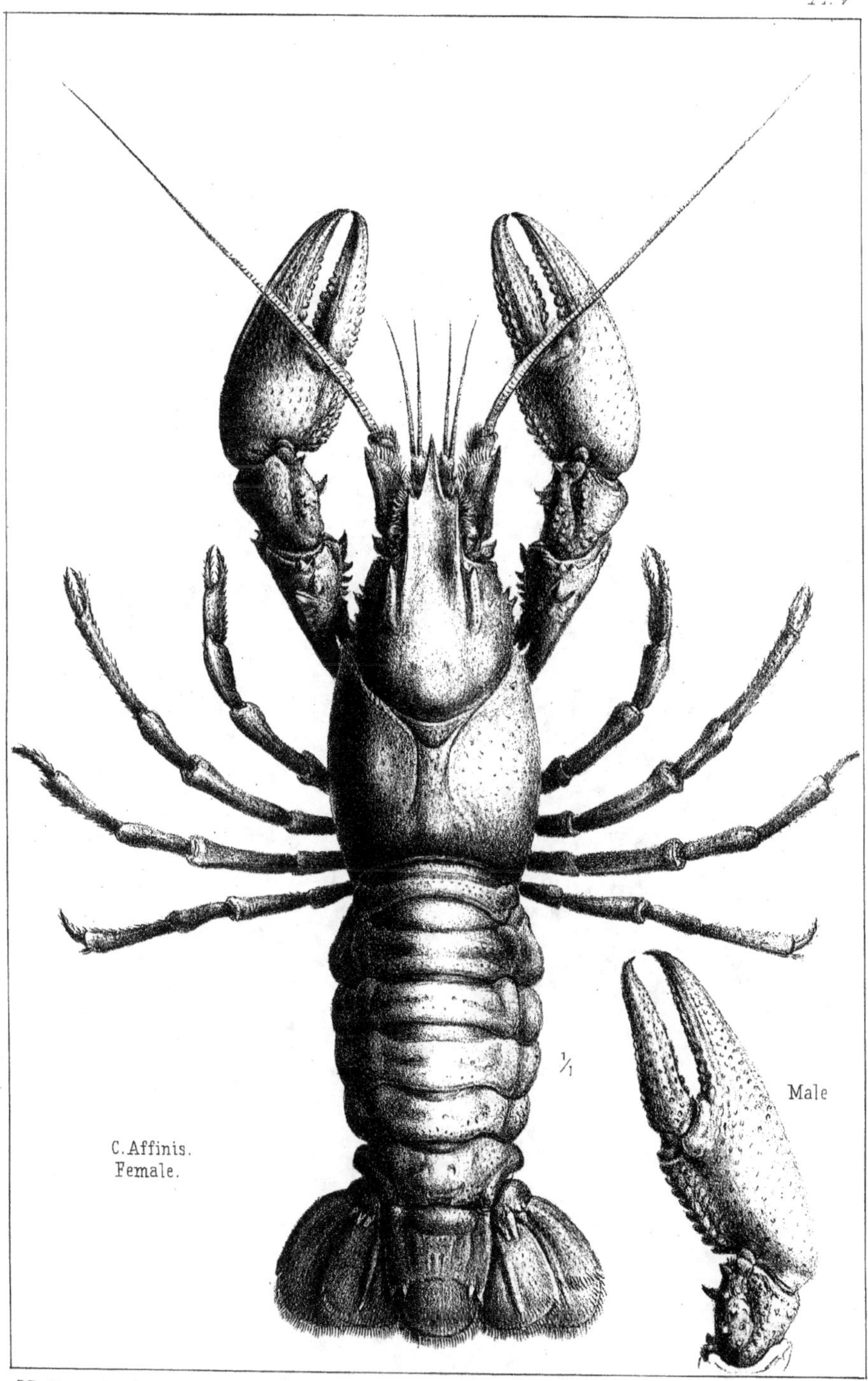

P. Roetter, on stone from nat.

New Eng. Lith. Co. Boston.

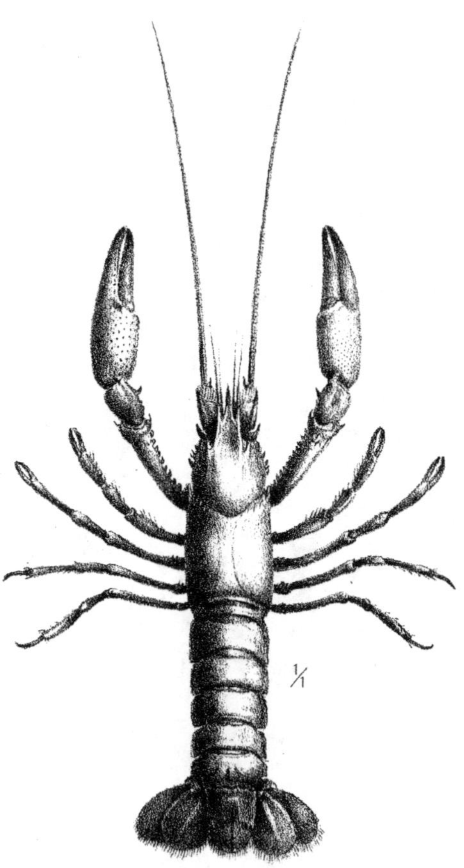

C. pellucidus Male. Form I.

P. Roetter, on stone from nat.

New Eng. Lith. Co. Boston.

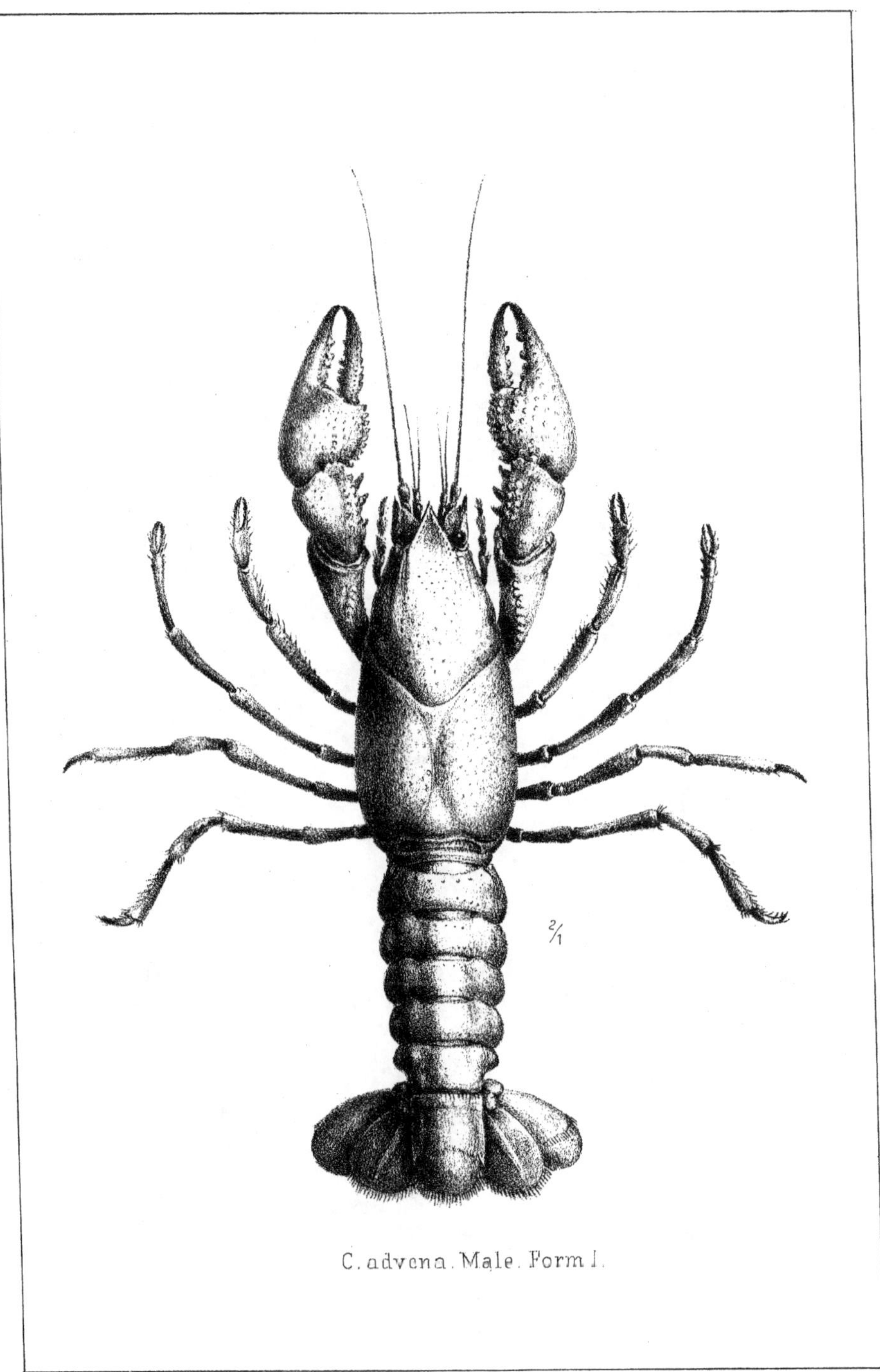

C. advena. Male. Form I.

P. Roetter, on stone from nat.

New Eng. Lith. Co. Boston.

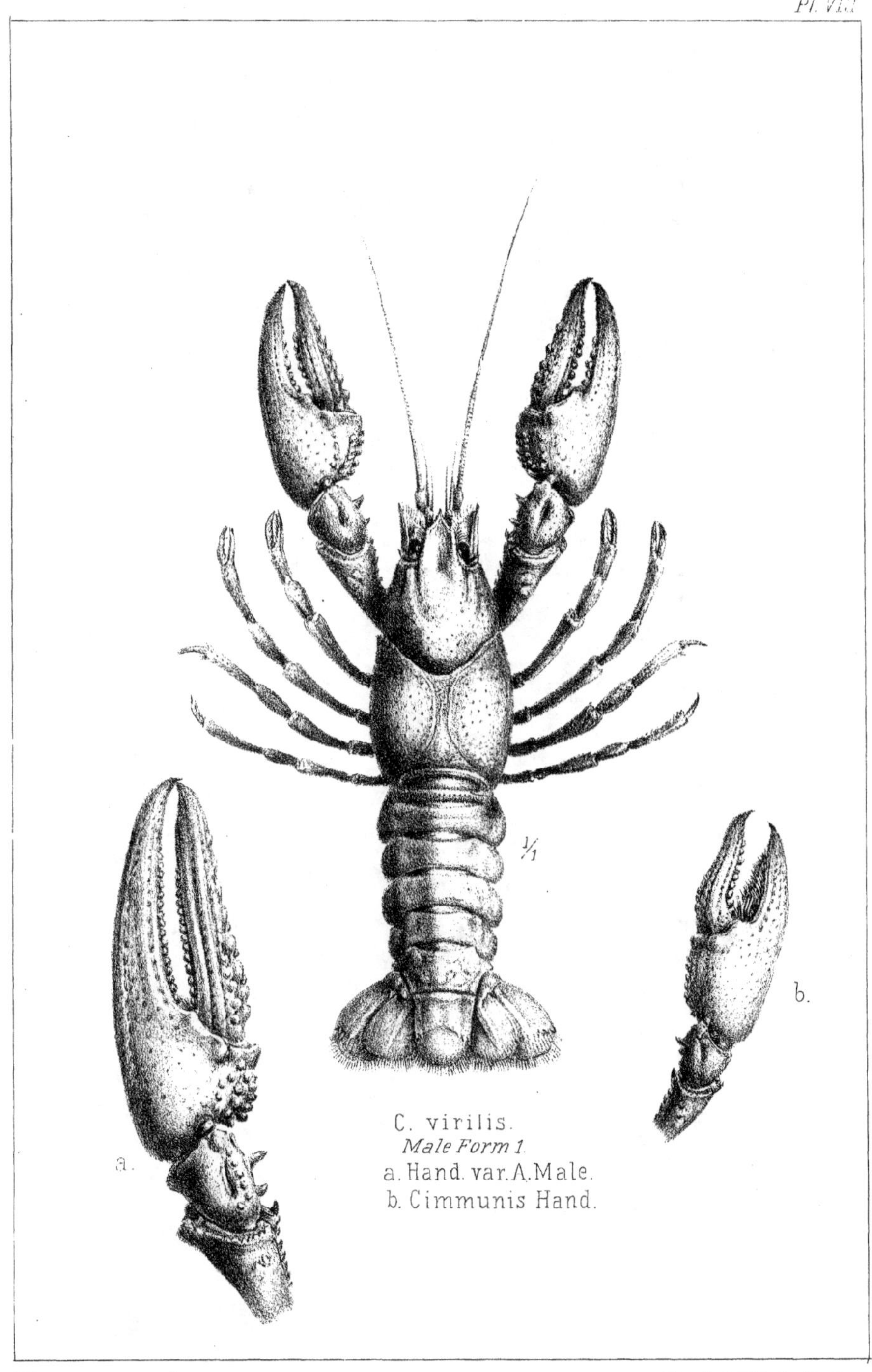

C. virilis.
Male Form 1.
a. Hand. var. A. Male.
b. Cimmunis Hand.

P. Roetter on stone from nat. New Eng. Lith. Co. Boston.

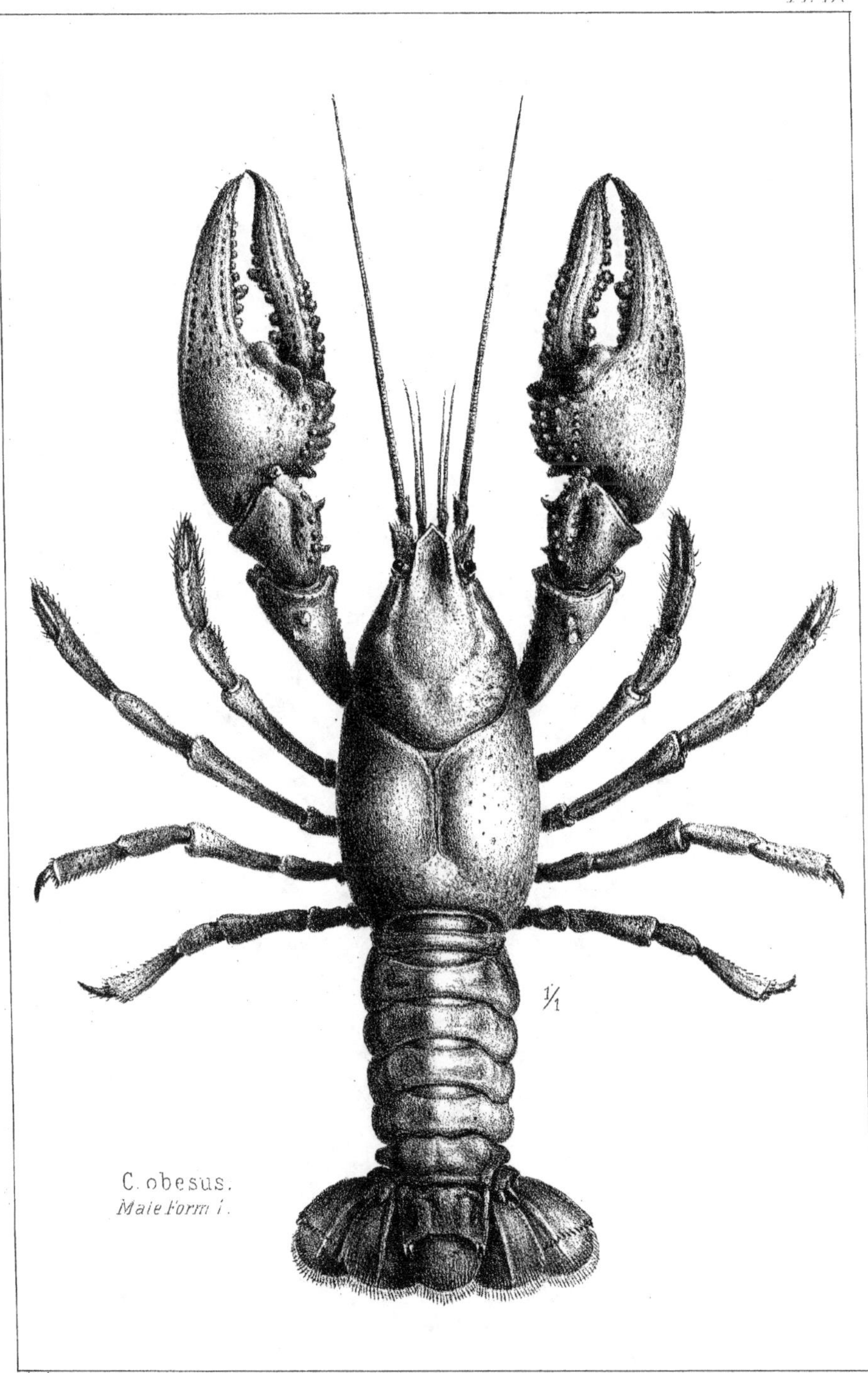

C. obesus.
Male Form I.

P. Roetter, on stone from nat. New Eng. Lith. Co. Boston.

A. Trowbridgii. Female.

P. Roetter, on stone from nat. New Eng. Lith. Co. Boston.

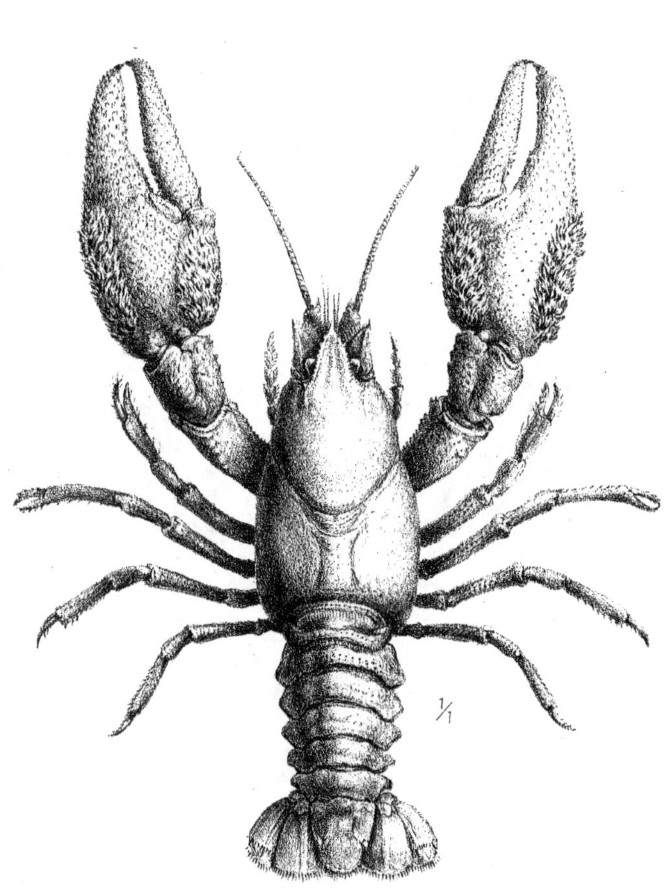

A. Gambelii. Male.

P. Roetter, on stone from nat

New Eng. Lith. Co. Boston.

www.ingramcontent.com/pod-product-compliance
Lightning Source LLC
LaVergne TN
LVHW021411110826
845150LV00007B/1882

* 9 7 8 1 4 2 5 5 1 0 7 6 3 *